Luigi Novelli

Shanghai

Architecture Guide

上海建筑百年

Haiwen Audio-Video Publishers

Contents

Acknowledgements

Thanks to Shanghai Book Traders

Special thanks for translation and editing to:

Ms. Claudia Albertini

Ms. Lisa Chisolm

Mr. Eric Lock

Mr. Luo Weiguo

Ms. Daniela Pilia

Preface:

Criteria and Comments

This book is a guide to architecture. This series of guides follows a consistent concept, illustrating buildings with photos, drawings and details of their location in the city. Each structure has the same amount of space devoted to it. Photos are the same size — an exterior view and others showing details or interiors. Text and photos must be explicit: they are not emphatic or vice versa unfavorable.

No personal comments or opinions are included in the guides.

These guides illustrate the architecture and urban landscape in the form of a snapshot from the 1990s to the beginning of the 21st century, which is the period of Shanghai's (second) huge transformation.

Due to the huge scale of the city — 16 million inhabitants — and the large quantity of architecturally interesting buildings, I had to make choices. I needed some guiding criteria.

I followed these criteria: cultural heritage, designers and architects, representativeness, location and dimensions. The result is a combination of all of them.

a) Cultural Heritage: I obtained information about the most interesting buildings and those under the protection of the law from books by professors at Tongji University.

b) Designers and architects: Chinese architects, Chinese architectural institutes and foreign architects designed most of the buildings in the city. Other examples lack details of the designers (especially Longtang houses, warehouses, etc.). In some cases, it is not necessary to mention the designers, especially for residential houses.

c) Representativeness: some examples are chosen because they represent a certain theory or trend. Such examples should not be too different from the ideas they are chosen to represent.

d) Location: this is a difficult factor to evaluate. But there is no doubt that buildings in key locations and on main roads — especially public ones — are representative of ideas, concepts and taste. As it was in the past with the waterfront Bund, so it is nowadays with People's Square, Pudong Lujiazui, the Huangpu riverfront, Hongqiao New Area, Xintiandi and other districts that are representative and symbolic of the architecture throughout the city.

e) Dimensions: also difficult to evaluate. But there is no doubt that the dimensions of buildings are representative of ideas, concepts and taste. However, the former RAS Bldg. in

Huqiu Road — one of the smallest buildings documented, located in a remote street — is one of the most interesting buildings in Shanghai. I have also considered and mentioned the Brilliant City beside the Suzhou River.

f) I considered only existing and completed buildings — except for a few under construction. I have not mentioned competitions, projects and other theories.

Since 1992, thanks to my job and this project, I have visited and lived in many residences in Shanghai, both in the Chinese and expatriate communities. Sometimes I rented the houses. I have stayed in the homes of my friends and relatives. I know the living situation in Shanghai and its social and technical problems: the inadequacies of the original construction techniques, overcrowding and the lack of sewage systems. I have seen situations similar to Italy in the 1950s, or London and Paris in the 19th century. Because of my background in history, I don't have — and I must not have — any sentimental feelings about this architecture. I am aware of the great improvements in housing since the 1950s in Shanghai and China. On the other hand, I know of the luxurious and wealthy residences of both Chinese and foreigners, in the past and in the modern day. But such issues are beyond the main topic of this architecture series.

Besides these criteria, the opinions and architectural information included are obviously influenced by my cultural background and my job as an Italian architect (I graduated in my native Rome) and by my private life in Shanghai. These guides are founded mainly on my research about Shanghai since 1997 and my personal experiences in the city since 1992. During the 1990s, I witnessed the rapid transformation of the city, I visited some important buildings when they were under construction — the Grand Theatre, the Jinmao Tower, the Xintiandi Area and the Bank of China in Beijing.

In Shanghai, Western architecture — both in the past and in recent times — is quite different from its roots in Europe and often lacks many elements of its original heritage. Chinese architecture, both traditional and modern, is not my cultural background. The combination of the two is the most interesting — and historically significant — aspect of Shanghai, and the most original and innovative aspect of this city's development.

Due to my background and experiences, the guides will focus primarily on the mixture of Chinese and Western architecture in Shanghai.

Luigi Novelli

Shanghai, September 2002

Preface:

Shanghai: Urban Development and New Architecture

Since 1992 Shanghai has been changing rapidly. It is a new city, just 150 years old. In the past, it has developed without a strong urban plan. Shanghai is a port and a trading centre.

Shanghai was founded and grew up as a point of encounters between Chinese and foreigners (British, Americans, French, Germans, Japanese, etc.) and there were foreign concessions under colonial rule.

Today it is once more the point where China meets the West. This explains its variety of architectural styles, ways of erecting buildings, methods and theories of town planning. It is studded with new buildings manned by architects, engineers, planners and technicians from all over the world.

Shanghai has been called China's most Westernised City, and this explains some of its distinctive urban features. But this is not all true. The city's urban pattern mainly is not based on the relationship between solids (the buildings) and voids (the streets) as the Western tradition. Shanghai is a hybrid city, neither Chinese nor Western.

The most interesting aspects of the city is the way Western and Chinese traditions of buildings integrate with each other, forming a combination of different types of buildings which leave a deep impression on visitors.

The mixture between Western and Chinese architecture was fully displayed in Shanghai. The meeting between the two civilizations could produce unexpected and surprising results as it happened in similar situation during the centuries. The most interesting aspects of this process is how and with which methods Western and Chinese construction traditions can be integrated, despite the evident differences between the two. There is no doubt that this process is already taking place.

Shanghai, a Hybrid Contemporary City

In Shanghai today there are almost all the architectural ideas and city concepts of the last century and even before, both Western and Chinese. In the same area many different styles and city concepts overlap one another. Sometimes blended, sometimes clashed. Shanghai is a hybrid city, a museum of world architecture.

There is the old Chinese traditional architecture in the Yu Yuan Garden and in Longhua Temple, Longhua Pagoda, Jade Buddha Temple, Jing'an Temple. There is the contemporary reconstruction in traditional style too, as the Market Area in the Old City and the Longhua New Town. There is the Neo-classic Chinese style in the Government buildings in Yangpu District built in the 1930s.

From houses in Longtangs, one can see many different styles: European styles like Spanish and Mediterranean or Alpine; Rationalist; Wright like architecture; Renaissance style architecture; mixed Spanish-Chinese and over all mixed Western and Chinese.

In the historical public buildings many are in different Western styles too. The Neo-classic style in the Shanghai Pudong Development Bank, the Children's Palace, the former French Sports Club, the Lyceum, the City Hall, Pacific Hotel, and Shanghai Mint Building; the Eclectic style in the General Post Office Building on the north bank of Suzhou Creek and in the former Library now Shanghai Art Museum; the Norwegian style in the Moller House; the Modernist in the Park Hotel, the Shanghai Mansion, the Grosvenor House, the Zhonghui Building, the Jialing Building built in the 1930s; the Rationalistic architecture in the Wu's House.

The Soviet style is seen in the Shanghai Exhibition Centre in the 1950s.

The socialistic architecture is seen in the numerous residential housing compounds and other public institutions such as hospitals, universities and schools built since the 1950s.

The new public buildings are the best examples of contemporary Chinese architecture, they include those in the People's Square — Shanghai Museum, City Hall and the Urban Planning Exhibition Centre, the Municipal Library and the Oriental Pearl TV Tower. Also the buildings by the architecture institutes of Shanghai are symbolic examples of modern Chinese architecture: the three Broadcasting Buildings, one in Hongqiao Area and others in Pudong New Area and in the center of the city.

The modern Western architecture can be seen in the numerous new high-rises and residential buildings built since 1992. International Style, Post-Modern, Le Courbusier-like architecture, the "engineering esthetic", the high-tech British architecture, etc. Furthermore the buildings by the two American architecture studios — KPF and HOK — represent the new contemporary international architecture worldwide — from USA to Europe, from South America to Sydney or Shanghai.

Architecture and City between China and the West

Among all of these styles there are the mixed ones, between the West and China: this is a real hybrid style, even impossible to give it a name.

The first examples are built by the Americans or British from the late 19th Century.

The most famous is the former St. John's University (now the East China University of Politics & Law) built from 1897 to 1905. The main three storied building, the Taofeng Hall (former SY

Hall) has a Western layout with a courtyard surrounded by a portico with a small tower in the centre. The Chinese elements are in the south/north main axis and southward entrance facing, the curved roof and the exterior pattern of bricks.

In the 1930s the small former RAS Building, the YMCA Building, the YWCA Building and the building of Bank of China are the most interesting mixed and hybrid examples.

In the 1990s the Shanghai Portman Centre, the Garden Hotel, the Shanghai Grand Theatre and the Jinmao Building are the most significant examples of mixed architecture.

On the other hand, many Western style buildings are influenced by the Chinese layout rules. Their main important axis is the south/north one so that the buildings all face south — the entrance, the main rooms and, most importantly, the facade itself. Although the styles of the buildings are Western these kind of construction are hybrid, they are not anymore Western architecture. Buildings as the Children's Palace, the Wu's House, the Shanghai Mint Building, the French Sports Club of the 1920s and 1930s, the Shanghai Exhibition Centre in the 1950s and the Garden Hotel, the Shanghai Portman Centre, the new Shanghai Grand Theatre and all the international style buildings by Palmer&Turner of the 1990s are facing south.

The most interesting mixed and hybrid examples in the 1930s — as the small former RAS Building, the YMCA Buildings and the Bank of China — have both features, Chinese and Western, both in architecture styles and in lay-out planning. They are facing the street — the main facade and entrance — not the sun (as the Chinese tradition). The YMCA Building has relation both with the street and the sun: the facade is along the street and the internal courtyard faces south.

In the 1990s, the Jinmao Building has both features, Chinese and Western, both in architecture styles and in layout planning.

Shanghai: a Modern Chinese City

Following the rigid Chinese rules, many buildings have only the Western styles but not their architectural concepts. In these cases the building's layout and the exterior style are separated, there is a dichotomy between the building and its facade. The style is only an exterior surface. No matter what is the function, the technologies, the construction period of the buildings, they can be "covered" with any style. It is not the Western styles of the buildings in Shanghai that make Shanghai a Western city.

In the Western style buildings facing south there is a mono-directional axis so that they completely lack the multi-direction axis, features of Western architecture. This means that they lack — first of all — the dynamism innate in the history of Western architecture. So that they lack the freedom of Western architecture ideas too. The mono-directional axis means a static layout: both features of Chinese tradition.

The mono-directional axis and the static layout cause the terraced and aligned plans in the

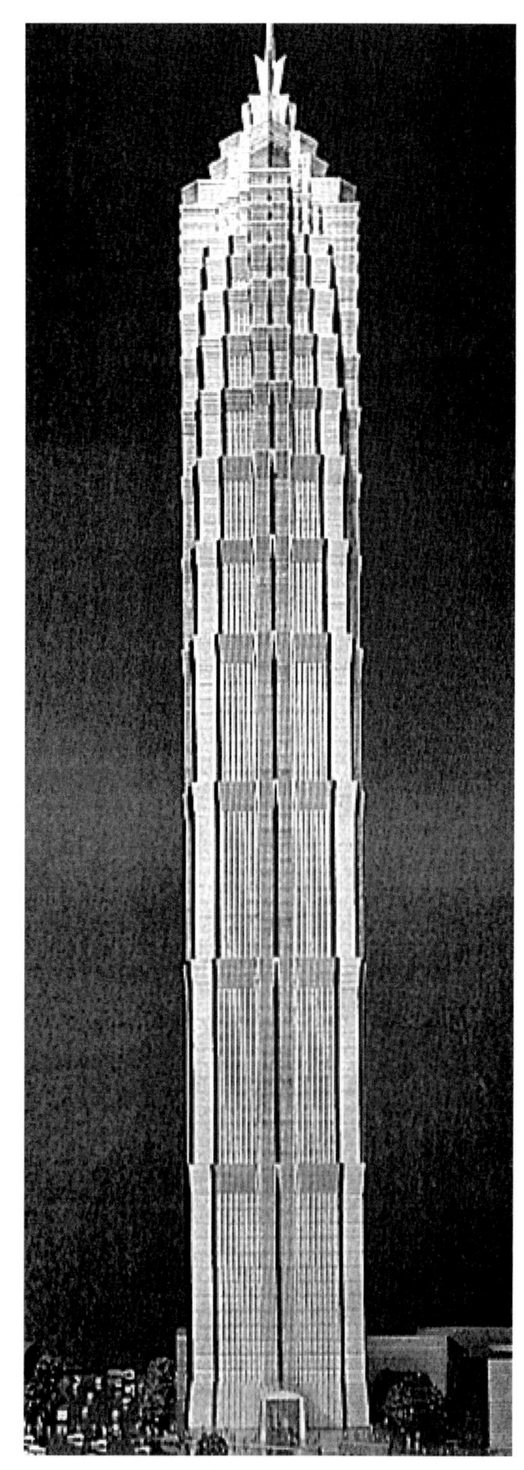

Jinmao Tower

city planning too. The city's urban pattern is not based on the relationship between solids — the buildings — and voids — the streets and squares. "Terraced" and "aligned" constructions have their main facade and main entrance pointing to the same direction. In these construction blocks, the most important element is the very orientation of the buildings. This means that they "must" be aligned and parallel. There is no urban relation between them. In Chinese tradition there is no such thing as a "facade" and the streets are thus not an architectural backdrop. Perspective constructions do not exist at all, too. There is no tradition of "urban space" in Chinese history.

People's Square — the core of modern Shanghai — is not an urban space based on the relationship between solids — the four public buildings — and voids — the area between them.

Many public buildings have no relation with the city either in the past or in recent times: buildings such as the Children's Palace, the Wu's House, the Shanghai Mint Building, the French Club House, the Grosvenor House, the Jinjiang Hotel built in the 1920s and 1930s; the Garden Hotel, the Shanghai Portman Centre and the new high-rise buildings designed by Palmer&Turner in the 1990s. They don't create any urban spaces. They all point southwards following the Chinese tradition, without any regards for city planning.

The Longtang houses layout comes from the Chinese tradition too, no matter what their exterior styles are. The houses are aligned and terraced all pointing at the same direction: the south.

On the other hand, the Bund/Waitan with the Shanghai Mansion, the Hamilton crossroads, the stretch of Nanjing Lu north of People's Square (the No.1 Department Store, the Pacific Hotel, the Shanghai Sports Club, the Park Hotel and the Grand Theatre) in the past and the new areas of Hongqiao and Pudong in these days are the only real urban spaces in the city (due to the relation between the buildings and the streets).

Other Western buildings both in the past and in the recent times have a relation with the city's plan so as to create urban space even if limited between the front and the opposite area. The theatres facing the streets as the Lyceum Theatre, the City Hall Theatre, the Cathay Theatre and the Majestic Theater; the Paramount Ballroom; the Zhonghui Building; the General Post Office and the Embankment Building along the Suzhou Creek in the 1920s and 1930s. In these days the Gee House in Hengshan Lu; the Jiushi Building in the south Bund; the Plaza 66 in Nanjing Xi Lu are some examples.

Some modern Chinese architecture buildings have a relation with the city layout too, like the Municipal Library in Huaihai Lu, the three broadcasting buildings, some high-rises in Hongqiao Area and others in Pudong New Area. These buildings merged the contemporary Chinese architecture with the Western city concepts.

In Hongqiao and Pudong new areas the buildings have different layout and orientations, usually relating to the streets, so as to create urban spaces and dynamic perspectives.

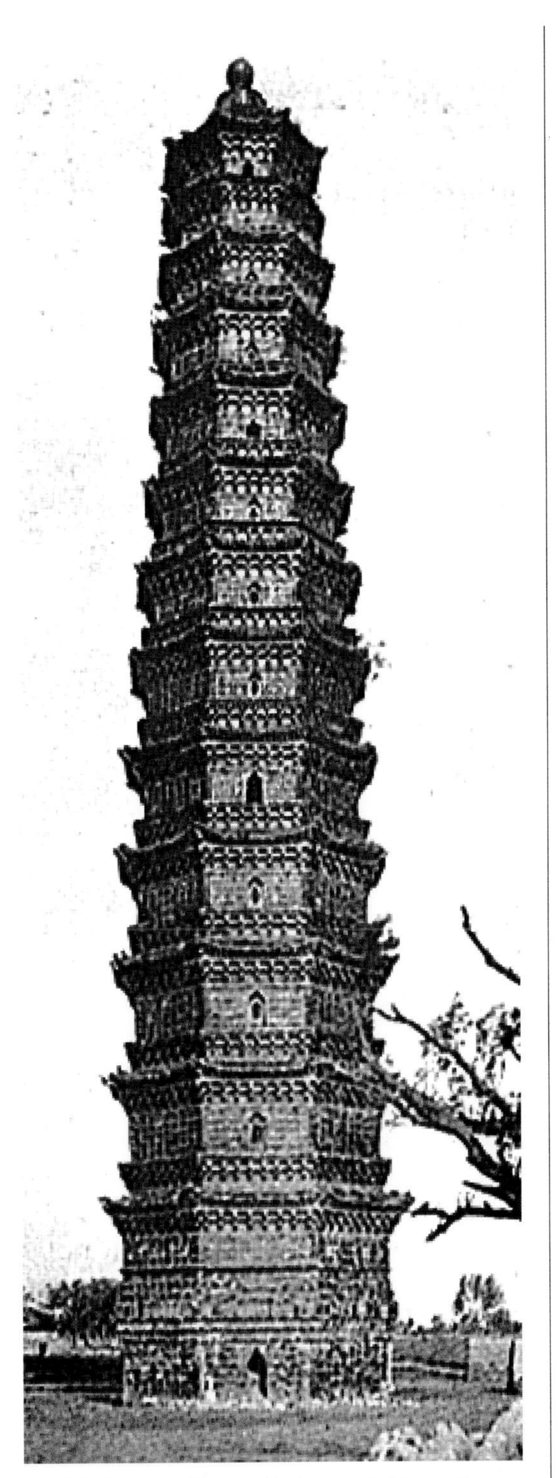

Kai Feng Iron Coloured Pagoda

The city is like an "Exhibition of Fun Fair Architectures"

In architecture the dichotomy between the building and its facade — in other words, the style is like an exterior surface — means there is no relation between interior and exterior spaces. This means no research about the architectural spaces.

The style is like an exterior surface, making itself the most important feature of the building, so that they can be used separated from their roots and meaning. The buildings became much more especially a sign or a landmark to be impressed in the memories of inhabitants. All of this means that the architecture could be a joke and the city could be an amusement city.

This is what is going to happen in many cities among the world, from Las Vegas to Tokyo.

Also the reconstruction of Shanghai in the 1990s — of course greatly influenced by 20th century's world trends — and as a consequence of its history like a hybrid city (or an "architectural fair") makes the metropolis like an "amusement park".

Intentionally Shanghai wants to make an impression on both inhabitants and visitors.

In Las Vegas, Nevada USA, since the 1950s each hotel has a "theme" and a consequential style: the Roman Empire theme in the Caesar Palace Hotel, the Venetian Hotel, the New York Hotel, the Paris Hotel, the Arizona Hotel, the Italian Lake Bellagio Hotel, the ancient Egypt Hotel, The Treasure Island Hotel, etc. The buildings recall the atmosphere of those environments.

In the Disneyland Amusement Parks, where the cities in the cartoons are reconstructed for entertainment, the concepts are similar to Las Vegas. The hotels, designed by architect M. Graves, have the same shape of the Disney characters.

In both situations the buildings recall something else somewhere else. In both situations the amusement buildings have to make an impression on the visitors.

The discotheques all over the world follow the same ideas to create an impressive interior design, too. Also the cinema's effects, the TV stages influenced whatever outside the performance environments. Furthermore the colorful children's toys and their assemblage have their influence on the architecture ideas too.

Following Las Vegas — as about twenty-five years ago architect Robert Venturi wrote in his work: *Learning from Las Vegas* — and following also cinemas and TV performances, the children's toys, the Disneyland Parks, new elements entered into the architecture tradition. Something that in the past very seldom joined it. The colour effects, the light effects, the plying of the fountains, the fireworks, the advertising posters, the matching of different materials and colours, etc. join now the construction not only as "accessories". At the same time, the style and the main facade both acquire a great importance and they become independent from the building.

Furthermore since the 1980s the Post-Modern architecture — starting in the USA — used the classic language elements of Western architecture as a joke, intentionally not following the traditional rules.

Nowadays the reconstruction and the huge transformation of Shanghai — and even the existing ones — are greatly influenced by the world's cities' development of the previous decades.

The Longtang Houses — like a movie set depending on their styles — recall the workers housing in England during the Industrial Revolution, the European Alpine valleys, the French and Spanish Mediterranean Riviera, the French Alsazia wooden frame houses, etc. The renovation of Longtang Houses in Xintiandi Area, changing completely the function from residential to entertainment, makes the whole complex as a stage for TV and movie performances.

The reconstruction in Chinese traditional style of new streets and new buildings in the Market City Old Town and Longhua New Town — joined with the original ones — makes the whole two complexes an atemporal "Chinese Amusement Park".

The pedestrian Huangpu River tunnel from Bund/Waitan to the Oriental Pearl TV Tower with the colourful light effects and the loudly music resembles a disco internal space.

The numerous different tops of the high-rise buildings — pyramid, sphere, crown, cusp shape, etc. — make the skyline like a cartoon-futuristic city.

The re-styling of the Railway Station building — from socialistic one to international high-tech — could change whenever it's necessary, the building remains always the same.

The two skyscrapers by J. Portman are both impressive architecture: Tomorrow Square on the west side of the People's Square is like a stone rocket. The Bund Financial Tower final project is like a huge flower. (The Bund Financial Tower's first project was not so impressive: it was an international style building.)

The Jin Mao internal top open space — from the 50th floor to the 85th floor — is much more an awful huge well than a real architectural space.

So that — in the urban scale — the People's Square and the Science City open-air empty spaces are much more non-human scale esplanades than real squares.

The mixed architecture itself — matching Western and Chinese elements — could seem a playful architecture.

Nowadays Shanghai city both historical and modern — the Old Chinese city, the Bund/Waitan, the Pudong New Area, the Longhua New Town, the People's Square — has the most impressive image during the night. The light effects reflecting on the waters mix up everything and sponge out any architectural imprecision or vice versa emphasize architectural jokes.

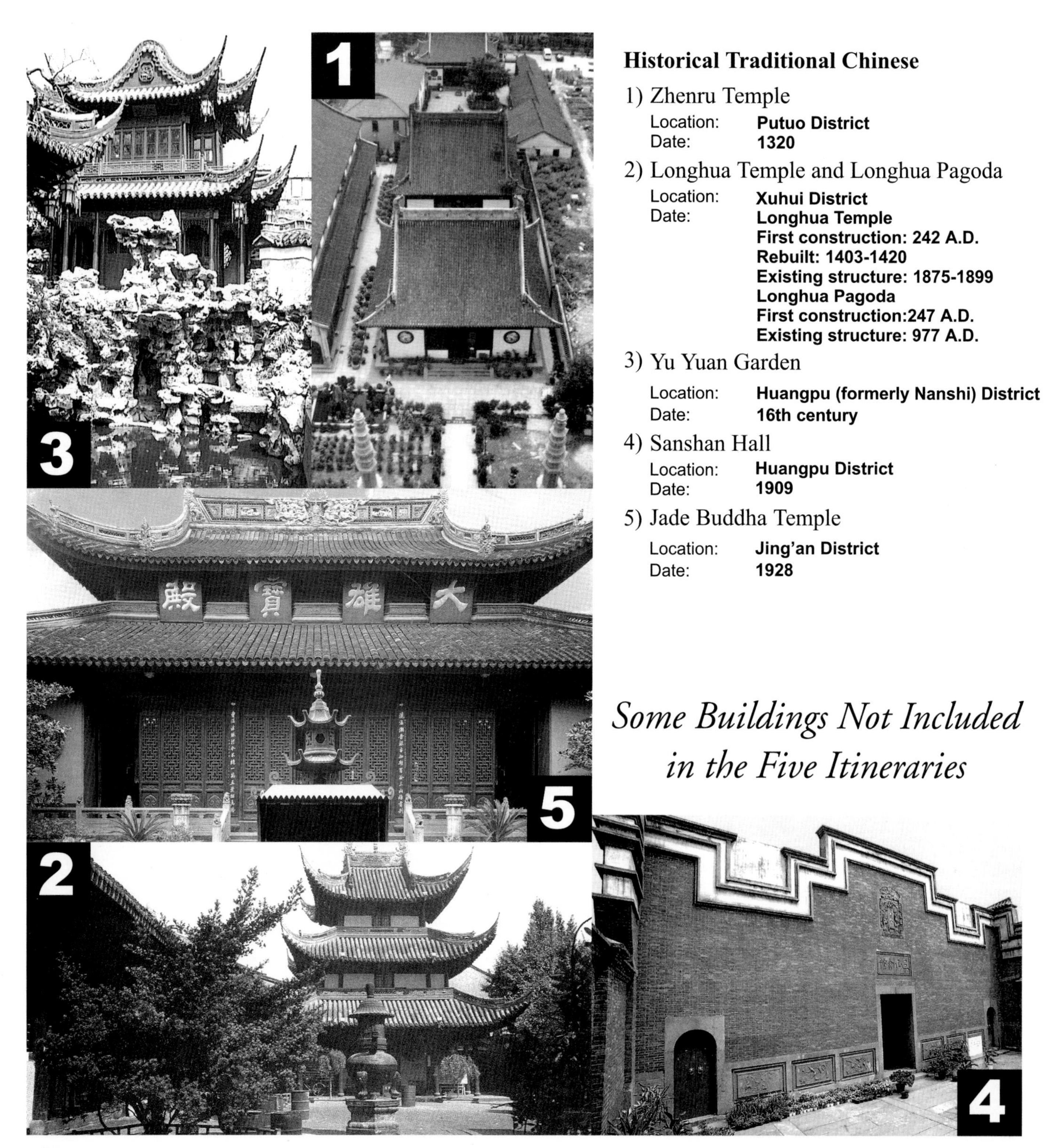

Historical Traditional Chinese

1) Zhenru Temple

Location:	**Putuo District**
Date:	**1320**

2) Longhua Temple and Longhua Pagoda

Location:	**Xuhui District**
Date:	**Longhua Temple**
	First construction: 242 A.D.
	Rebuilt: 1403-1420
	Existing structure: 1875-1899
	Longhua Pagoda
	First construction:247 A.D.
	Existing structure: 977 A.D.

3) Yu Yuan Garden

Location:	**Huangpu (formerly Nanshi) District**
Date:	**16th century**

4) Sanshan Hall

Location:	**Huangpu District**
Date:	**1909**

5) Jade Buddha Temple

Location:	**Jing'an District**
Date:	**1928**

Some Buildings Not Included in the Five Itineraries

Modern Buildings

1) East China University of Politics and Law

(Formerly St. John's University)
Location: **Changning District**
Date: **1894/1927**

2) Kadoorie House (Now Children's Palace)
Location: **Jing'an District**
Date: **1924**

3) General Post Office
Location: **Hongkou District**
Date: **1924**

4) Pacific Hotel
Location: **Huangpu District**
Date: **1926**

5) Hongde Church
Location: **Hongkou District**
Date: **1924**

6) Shanghai Mint Building
Location: **Putuo District**
Date: **1929**

7) Moller House
Location: **Xuhui District**
Date: **1936**

8) Shanghai Exhibition Centre
Location: **Jing'an District**
Date: **1955**
See Itinerary 4-1

7

Grand Theatre in 1930s

Itinerary 1

Shanghai in the 1930s

The city's great period of expansion that had begun midway through the 19th century reached its peak in the 1930s, and was only halted by the Japanese occupation in August 1937. The city had been under colonial rule with the establishment of the foreign concessions (British in 1846, American in 1848, French in 1849, Japanese in 1866). The population leapt up from 500,000 in 1850 to around 5, 000,000 in 1949.

In 1845 the *Land Law* established the separation of Chinese and non-Chinese residences and dwellings. These historical events have left their marks on the layout of the city, which was largely built by foreigners. The urban structure, architectural languages and above all the city culture are directly influenced by the city's historical development, causing Shanghai to be viewed as China's most westernized city. In the 1990s, with Shanghai (now an independent Municipality with a burgeoning population of 15,000,000) undergoing a rapid and radical building transformation, the part of the city built in the period from the end of the last century to the 1930s may be considered as the historical centre resulting from its cultural uniqueness. This part is characterized by the street plan of the old foreign concessions — Beijing Lu, Nanjing Lu, Yan'an Lu, Huaihai Lu, People's Square — the core of Huangpu District, the Longtang dwellings and finally the Bund / Waitan (German and Chinese terms respectively) waterfront looking onto the river Huangpu. This urban layout was essentially western in style, based on the relationship between streets and buildings, regardless of the inclusion of traditional Chinese elements.

The old Chinese city, once enclosed within city walls, located to the south of the Huangpu District and easily identifiable owing to its circular layout, together with some temples that have now been incorporated into the urban fabric, make up the city's other historical centre, whose roots are firmly attached to the place itself.

The huge presence of foreigners (British, American, French, German, Japanese) has of course strongly influenced buildings and architectural trends, producing a vast range of styles (Western Neoclassical, Mediterranean Spanish, American Chicago school, Japanese, Hindu, English Gothic, traditional Chinese, European colonial). Individual architectural languages appear unrelated to either the type of building (multistorey buildings, dwellings and apartments, cinema/ theaters) or the structural technology adopted (usually reinforced concrete, with brickwork for the outside walls of large building), born of western origin. The traditional Chinese style may be seen above all in the old Museum, the old Library, the old Council House and the old Stadium all by Dong Dayou during 1933/ 35 period, included in the 1929 City Plan outside the Foreign Concessions zone. This zone should be considered the Chinese city during that period.

Aside from individual solutions, there are some particularly significant zones in the city taken as a whole: e.g. the Bund / Waitan riverside area, forming a compact building district that has become a symbol of the city, took on its final physiognomy in the 1930s (a total of twenty-five buildings constructed from 1860 to 1937, now a protected area) and Longtang dwelling areas.

This itinerary illustrates significant examples of the contemporary architecture of those years, and sets out to study the mixture of Western and Chinese styles and integration between architectural languages through examples that have proved difficult to classify, that is when in the same building there are more or less obvious elements of different architectural schools of thoughts.

Itinerary 1

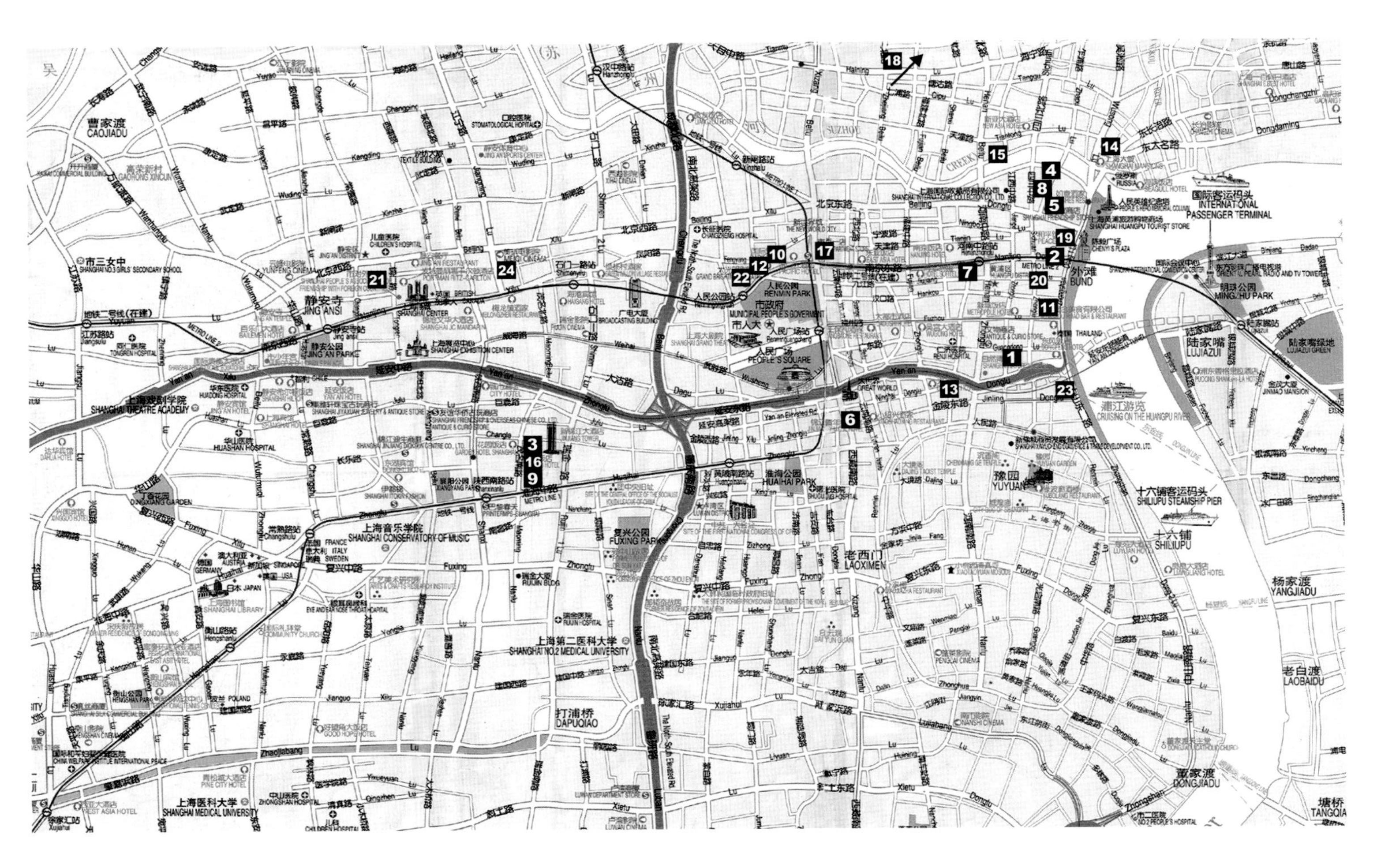
1
2
3
4
5
6
7
8
9
10
11
12
13
14
15
16
17
18
19
20
21
22
23
24
CAOJIADU
JING'ANSI
SHANGHAI THEATRE ACADEMY
PEOPLE'S SQUARE
RENMIN PARK
BUND
LUJIAZUI
YUYUAN
LAOXIMEN
FUXING PARK
HUAIHAI PARK
SHANGHAI CONSERVATORY OF MUSIC
SHANGHAI NO.2 MEDICAL UNIVERSITY
SHANGHAI MEDICAL UNIVERSITY
DAPUQIAO
DONGJIADU
SHILIUPU
YANGJIADU
LAOBAIDU
TANGQIAO
INTERNATIONAL PASSENGER TERMINAL
MINGZHU PARK
CRUISING ON THE HUANGPU RIVER
SHILIUPU STEAMSHIP PIER

1

SHANGHAI BUREAU OF LIGHT INDUSTRIES
上海轻工业局

(Shanghai Sports Club 1920; China Industrial Bank)

Date: 1920 (1931)
Design: E.Hazard
Function: Offices
Huangpu District
33, Sichuan Zhong Lu
黄浦区四川中路 33 号

The architect was the American E. Hazard. His works are marked by the alternating use of different materials or bricks of different colors, and by the division of the facade into alternating vertical strips (the solidity of the masonry and the emptiness of the windows set in close rows). A characteristic element is the metallic black covering, with flowery geometrical patterns, of spaces between the windows of one storey and another. The building's volume is line with the street and symmetrical. The same architect also designed the Shanghai Electric Power Building (1929), at 181, Nanjing Dong Lu.

The Peace Hotel is one of Shanghai's landmark buildings, standing out on the skyline among the compact building curtain of the Bund/Waitan. The Peace Hotel consists of a vast building with a triangular base, with a clear-cut hierarchy between the front, central and back parts. The front of the building, looking onto the river, rises to a tower and culminates in a pyramid. The two compact and uniform sides have three entrances, marked by a slight staggering of the facade. This division of the building into three distinct parts, the emphasis of the main face with the use of a tower (and balcony immediately below), the compactness and regularity of the terminal part of the sides are features found in other major buildings in Shanghai.

PEACE HOTEL
和平饭店

(Cathy Hotel)

Date: 1926/ 28
Design: Palmer & Turner
Function: Hotel
Huangpu District
20, Nanjing Dong Lu
黄浦区南京东路 20 号

2

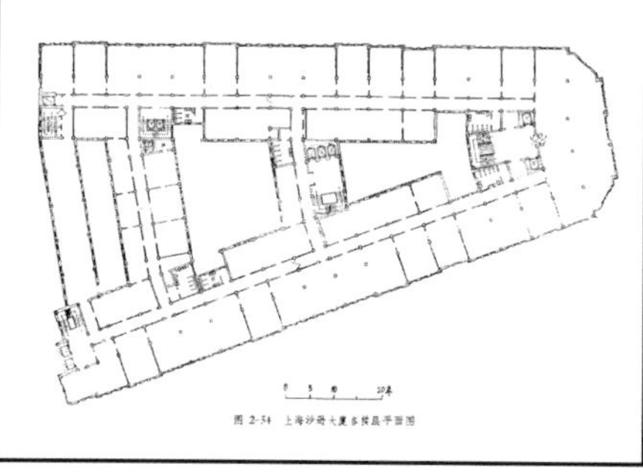

3

JINJIANG HOTEL NORTH BUILDING
锦江饭店北楼
(Cathay Mansion)

Date: 1925/29
Design: Algar and Co.
Function: Hotel
Luwan District
59, Maoming Nan Lu
卢湾区茂名南路 59 号

The Jiniang Hotel is a 13-storey building set apart from others, whose layout and shape are marked by two "T"s lying next to each other, with the continuous facade pointing southwards (according to Chinese tradition). The building's faces are characterized by the large partitioned windows and above all by the use of two prominent and contrasting colors: the white of the window frames, pilaster strips, cornices, the entire top floor and the wide joints between bricks and the bright red of the bricks themselves. The same colors were used by Davies and Brooke for the Lyceum Theatre in 1931, a building in Italian Renaissance style. The Jingjiang Hotel North Building brings to mind English Georgian architecture.

GUANGXUE BUILDING
广学大厦
(Christian Literature Society Building)

Date: 1930
Design: L.E.Hudeck
Function: Offices
Huangpu District
128, Huqiu Lu (209, Yuanmingyuan Lu)
黄浦区虎丘路 128 号(圆明园路 209 号)

4

The Czech architect L.E. Hudeck was one of the leading and most active architects in Shanghai in this period. His works are marked by a language and elements typical of contemporary Western architecture. It is a small building, looking onto two streets and a side lane. The main facade, in line with Huqiu Lu, has a large and tall pointed archway covered in concrete plaster. The higher storeys of the back of the building are terraced. The most significant elements are the characteristics of the building's facades: triangular pilaster strips between windows, having one or more tips, the red/brown of the brick, wide white brick joints, flower-stylized concrete capitals on top of the pilaster strips.

5

YWCA BUILDING

中华基督教女青年会会址

Date: 1930
Design: Li Jinpei (Poy Gum Lee)
Function: Offices
Huangpu District
133, Yuanmingyuan Lu
黄浦区圆明园路 133 号

An example of a blend of Chinese and Western styles. A small U-shaped building with the opening looking southwards according to Chinese tradition. The facade with main entrance is in line and looking onto the street. It is symmetrical in relation to the entrance, with the two ends of the building one storey higher. There is a long central terrace and the top two floors are set back. The long terrace and above all the width of the horizontal strips lend to the building a strong attachment to the ground, the horizontal axis being predominant despite the sides being divided into vertical strips. The entrance and geometric patterns of the horizontal strips are Chinese in style.

YMCA BUILDING

青年会宾馆

(Baxianqiao YMCA Building)
Date: 1931
Design: Li Jinpei,
Fan Wenzhao, Zhao Shen
Function: Hotel
Huangpu District
123, Xizang Nan Lu
黄浦区西藏南路 123 号

6

Li Jinpei (Poy Gum Lee), Fan Wenzhao (Robert Fan) and Zhao Shen are three Chinese architects that usually worked separately but came together for this project. The building is one of the most symbolic examples of the attempt to combine Chinese and Western architectural elements. The building respects the city plan alignment of the facade looking onto the street (from Western urban culture), while the U-shaped courtyard immediately behind the front of the building follows Chinese tradition, looking southwards. The front is characterized by two large cornices in Chinese style that highlight the top storey, containing large glazed windows and pillars (a prevalence of "empty" spaces typical of traditional Chinese architecture), and a tall slightly sloping three-storey base.

7

DONG HAI BUILDING

东海大楼

(Dalu Mall:
The Continental Emporium Building)
Date: 1931/ 32
Design: Zhuang Jun (T.Chuang)
Function: Department Store
Huangpu District
353, Nanjing Dong Lu (334, Jiujiang Lu)
黄浦区南京东路 353 号(九江路 334 号)

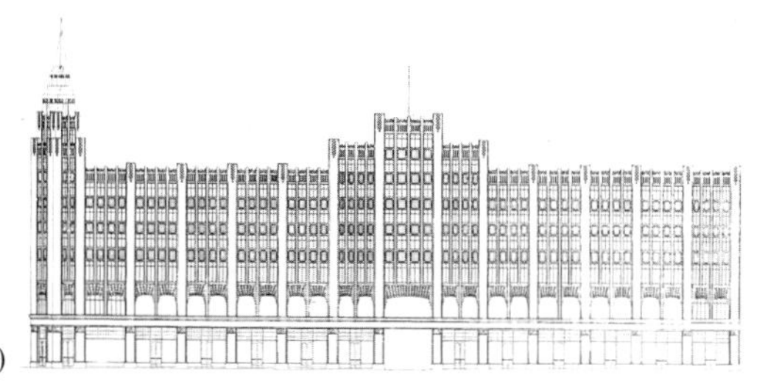

Large building looking out onto three streets designed by a Chinese architect in the absence of traditional Chinese elements. The north-facing front of the building, looking out onto the main street, Nanjing Lu, is compact and symmetrical in relation to the entrance, the south side looking onto Jiujiang Lu is terraced. There is a small tower on the corner of the facade looking over Naijing Lu. The emphatic horizontal nature of the building is offset by the equally emphatic verticality of the lines of the building facade. Interior has been renovated in the 1980s.

FORMER R.A.S.BUILDING

亚洲文会

北中国支会会址

(Royal Asiatic Society)
Date: 1932
Design: Plamer & Turner
Function: Offices
Huangpu District
20, Huqiu Lu
黄浦区虎丘路 20 号

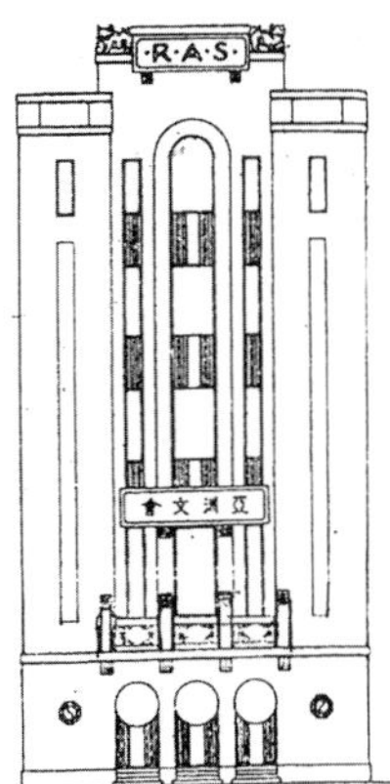

This is one of the most interesting and successful examples of integration between Western and Chinese elements, even though it was designed by non-Chinese architects. A small building in line with the street, its volume develops perpendicularly to the same street: the characteristic element is the facade looking onto the street. The red-bricked face is divided into three sections both vertically and horizontally: the base, setback of the central section, tall central arch, long vertical niches and eaves. The base, marked by a large balcony and two octagonal windows, and the eaves at the top are in Chinese style. The emphatic vertical nature of the building is offset by the weight of the base and the small detachment of the central section in relation to the sides at the top of the building, appearing to be a foretaste of the Bank of China building. The same architects designed the building at 50, Jiujiang Lu, an example of blended styles (stylized Corinthian/ Egyptian, Chinese decorations).

8

CATHAY THEATRE

国泰大戏院

Date: 1932
Design: C. H. Gonda
Function: Theatre-Cinema
Luwan District
870, Huaihai Zhong Lu (corner Maoming Nan Lu)
卢湾区淮海中路 870 号（茂名南路路口）

9

C.H. Gonda, the Hungarian architect, also designed the Guanglu Building, with auditorium/ cinema on the ground floor, in 1927 (146, ZhapuLu) and the Xinhua Cinema in 1939 (Nanjing Xi Lu, demolished in 1995). The entrance to the Cathay Theatre, situated on the corner of the two streets, is at a 45° angle to the crossroads, and has a south/ west exposure. The entrance facade is marked by vertical strips alternating with solid zones, formed by red facebricks having wide white joints, and narrow glazing with concrete frames. The front of the building rises at the centre to a pointed tower.

10

SHANGHAI SPORTS CLUB

上海体育俱乐部

(Foreign YMCA Building)
Date: 1926/33
Design: E.Hazard
Function: Offices
Huangpu District
150, Nanjing Xi Lu
黄浦区南京西路 150 号

Together with the Pacific Hotel, the Park Hotel and the Grand Theatre, this building formed (and continues to form) the built-up front on the northern side of the large open Hippodrome area, now the central square of Shanghai and the People's Park. The U-shaped building laid out on a single base is aligned and directed towards the street, looking southwards and towards the urban void. The central body farther from the street is taller. The facebricks are of different colors: yellow/brown and red/brown, laid in a diamond-shaped pattern. The vertical strips of the windows are made from dark brown bricks. The full vertical strips are sloping, and at the top they cross beyond the horizontal of the parapet, creating an emphatic battlement. The building takes on a European medieval appearance.

Twin buildings designed by the same architects and built one year apart. Their layout in relation to the crossroads takes the same shape as the previous building located there, the Shanghai Municipal Council Building of 1919, and is in turn taken up by the Development Building of Davies and Brooke Co., (1934) situated on the fourth corner of the crossroads. This is the only crossroads in Shanghai that has such a plan: all four neighboring buildings are set back in semicircular fashion and have their entrances on the same crossroads. Architecturally the two buildings are easily discernible thanks to the emphatic verticality of their lines, a higher central section rising up from the side wings, rectangular windows with longer vertical sides, a tower-like upper ridge and arches on top of the building, above the vertical columns of windows, both on the building body and on the face looking skywards.

11

FUZHOU BUILDING

(Hamilton House)

福州大楼

(汉弥登大厦)

Date: 1931/33

Design: Palmer &Turner

Function: Offices

METROPOLE HOTEL

新城饭店

(都城饭店)

Date: 1934

Design: Palmer & Turner

Function: Hotel

Huangpu District

170-180, Jiangxi Zhong Lu

(corner Fuzhou Lu)

黄浦区江西中路 170-180 号

（福州路路口）

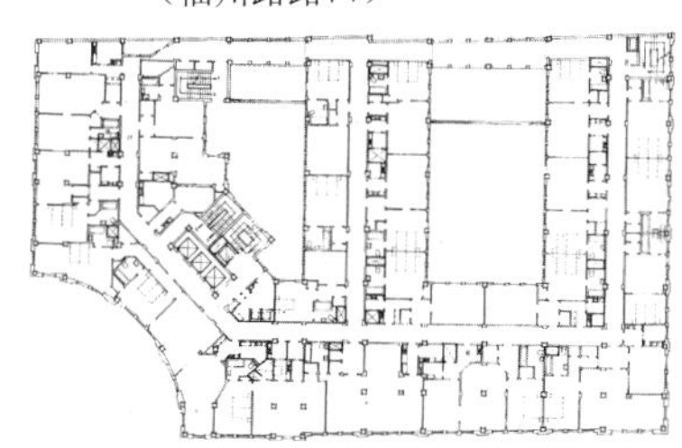

12

The Park Hotel is one of the most important historical buildings of Shanghai in terms of size and position. It was the highest building in the Far East until the 1980's (24 storeys). It was an architectural landmark in the extensive void of the Hippodrome, and although it is now dwarfed by the new skyscrapers it remains an impressive landmark on the northern side of the main square. It consists of a massive volume on a single base, with differences in the front, central body and back of the building as it rises up. The layout of the front of the building expands and rises up in tower form, with the facade looking onto the street, in a southward direction and towards the urban void. The sides are characterized by narrow vertical strips that (on the front face) rise up to the top of the tower, creating a sort of buttress. The windows set in rows are small and rectangular, with longer vertical sides. The pilaster strips are triangular. The red/brown covering is formed by square tiles laid at an angle of 45°and glazed bricks.

PARK HOTEL

国际饭店

Date: 1931/34

Design: L.E. Hudeck

Function: Hotel

Huangpu District

170, Nanjing Xi Lu

黄浦区南京西路 170 号

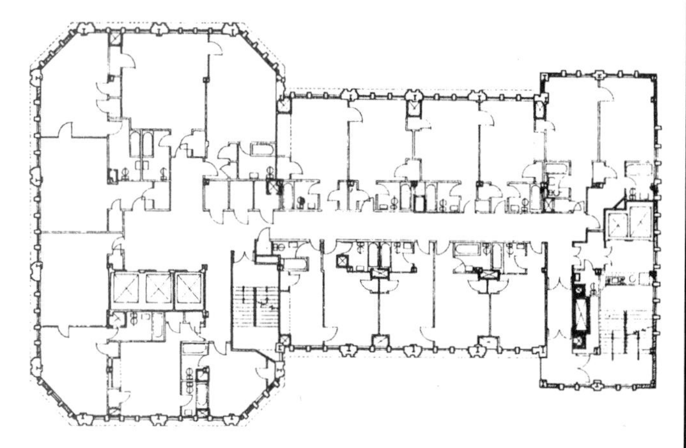

13

ZHONGHUI BUILDING
中汇大厦

Date: 1934
Design: A. Leonard, P. Veysseyre, M. Guillet
Function: Office
Huangpu District
16, Henan Nan Lu (corner Yan'an Lu)
黄浦区河南南路 16 号(延安路路口)

The architects worked mainly in the part of the city corresponding to the former French Concession, designing the French Sports Club in 1924 on Maoming Nan Lu, now the lobby of the Garden Hotel. The Zhong Hui Building is similar to other large buildings in Shanghai in terms of volume, formed by a front part, containing a pointed terraced tower, central body and back part, with a colonnade looking onto the street. It is pointed northwards, towards the main street. The facade has a convex curve with a balcony on the eighth floor, immediately below the tower section. Symmetrically midway along the sides of the building, there are two entrances highlighted by a column of balconies and raised eaves. Horizontal and vertical lines alternate. The Yan'an Lu overpass roadway built opposite the building in 1993/95 now prevents the facade from being seen in its entirety.

14

SHANGHAI MANSION (BROADWAY MANSION)
上海大厦(百老汇大厦)

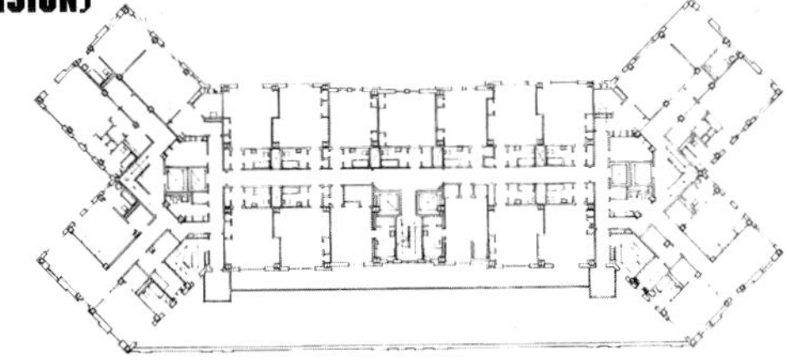

Date: 1934
Function: Hotel
Hongkou District
20, Bei Suzhou Lu
虹口区北苏州路 20 号

Shanghai Mansion is one of Shanghai's symbols, especially due to its position. It is one of the few buildings of city planning importance. It is the perspective pointer to the north of the Bund/Waitan riverside zone. The massive south-looking detached building (now surrounded by new taller buildings) is perpendicular to the long "building curtain" formed by the riverside area. The re-entering-wing plan (in this case double Y-shaped), the majestic terraced volume rising towards the centre (22 storeys), the facebricks (laid in different stages), the use of horizontal strips for the wings and vertical strips for the central body and ends render the building similar to the Hengshan Hotel and Grosvenor House, built in the same period. It was originally built to house apartment dwellings.

A large building for residential purposes situated on the northern bank of the Suzhou Creek, basically looking southwards. Three floors and the roof-terrace were added in the 1950s above the original eight storeys. The massive volume is characterized by the sweep of all its corners and by the presence of column-down loggias on all floors, alternating with solid walls containing windows. Sides are covered by concrete plaster and brown bricks (which originally created a battlement on the top of the building, cancelled out by the construction of the three upper floors). The predominantly horizontal nature of the building's lines, the low masonry parapet with several banisters and the alternating of solid and empty spaces of the corner loggias bring to mind the architecture of Mendhelsonn's great buildings. The courtyard is in a decentralized, open position facing south.

HEBING DALOU

(Embankment Building)

河滨大楼

Date: 1931/35

Design: Palmer & Turner
Function:Housing
Hongkou District
310/434, Bei Suzhou Lu
虹口区北苏州路 310-434 号

15

A large building similar to Shanghai Mansion: 19 storeys in the central part, 13 floors on the wings. Facing south/west. Its original (and current) use was to provide luxury housing (apartments, sometimes on two floors), causing the builders to take greater care over detail than for the Shanghai Mansion. Bricks laid first horizontally and then vertically, narrow vertical strips (pilaster) in white plaster in the central part and wings, geometric patterns on the architrave bring relief to the volume's mass. The same architects were responsible for the low buildings constructed along Maoming Nan Lu, called Grosvenor Gardens (now Jinjiang Hotel West Building).

16

JINJIANG HOTEL MIDDLE BUILDING

(Grosvenor House)

锦江饭店中楼

Date: 1934/35

Design: Palmer & Turner
Function: Housing
Luwan District
87, Maoming Nan Lu
卢湾区茂名南路 87 号

17

Impressive 11-story building with pointed corners. Continues and ends row of buildings on Nanjing Xi Lu including the Grand Theatre, Park Hotel, Shanghai Sports Club and Pacific Hotel on the northern side of the People's Square. The facade is base on vertical lines. The facebricks are yellow. The same architects designed the Zhongshan Hospital in traditional Chinese style in 1937 in 136, Yixueyuan Lu.

SHANGHAI NO.1 DEPARTMENT STORE

(Da Sun Department Store)

上海第一百货商店

Date: 1934/36
Design: Kwan, Chu, Yang
Function: Department Store
Huangpu District
830, Nanjing Dong Lu (corner Xizang Lu)
黄浦区南京东路 830 号（西藏路路口）

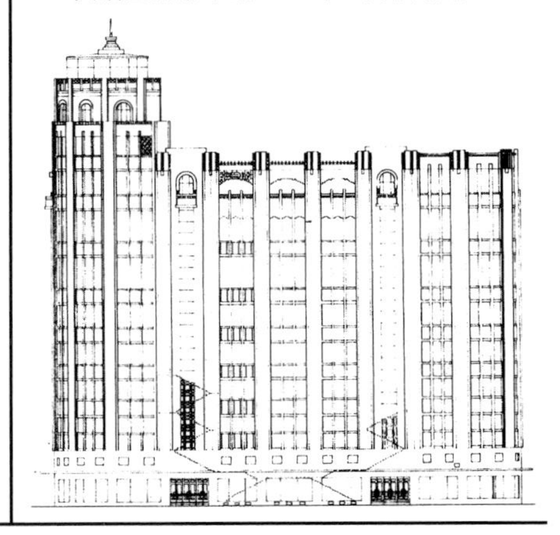

When the Foreign Concessions existed, the Municipal Government of Shanghai had a new civic centre, museum, library and stadium all included in the 1929 City Plan built outside the Foreign Concessions zone. Due to this concept, the style of these buildings had to be traditionally Chinese, "Palatial Chinese" or Neo-classic Chinese. The concrete structure comes from the modern and Western technologies so that the result is very different from the traditional Chinese wooden structure.

18

SHANGHAI INSTITUTE OF PHYSICAL CULTURE

上海体育学院办公楼

(former Shanghai Municipal Administration Building)
（大上海计划市政府大楼）
Date: 1934/36
Design: Dong Dayou
Function: Offices
Hongkou District
650, Qingyuan Huan Lu
虹口区清源环路 650 号

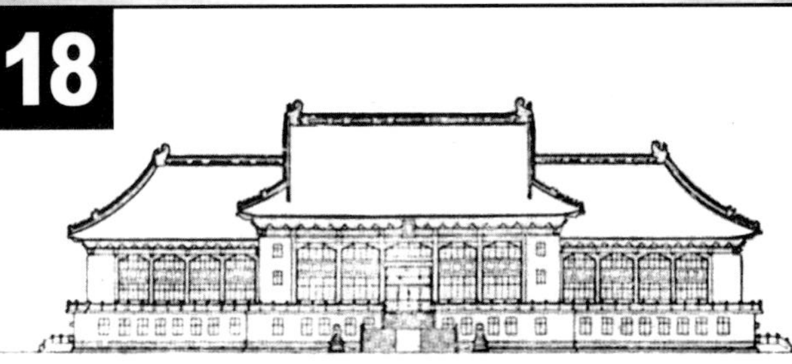

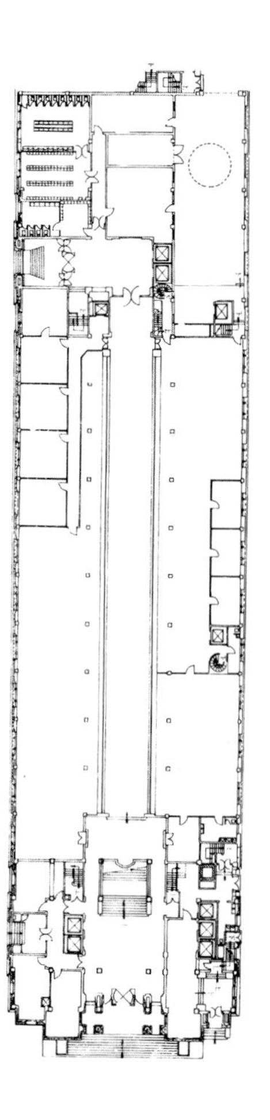

19

This, together with the Peace Hotel next to it, were Shanghai's most representative buildings, standing out on the riverside skyline. It is of special interest due to the attempt made to combine the Chinese style with modern-day western architectural languages. The building was designed jointly by Western and Chinese architects. It consists of two parts: the long and low back part and the 17-story riverside part. In the part containing the main tower there is a juxtaposition of parallelepiped parts that rise towards the central part. The main part looks onto the riverside avenue. The most evident Chinese elements are the stylistic details: the main doorway, the two columns of lattice face windows, the curved cornice at the top. The Chinese nature of the building also derives from the apparent weight of the building, the top of the building relatively undetached from the central part, thus neutralizing the verticality of the facade.

BANK OF CHINA

中国银行

Date: 1936/37

Design: Palmer &Turner Lu Qianshou (H.S. Luke)

Function: Offices

Huangpu District

23, Zhongshan Dong Yi Lu

黄浦区中山东一路23号

20

The volume of the Jialing Building is in keeping with other major buildings in Shanghai: a higher front, central body and back. Its layout is in line not with the main road, Nanjing Lu, but with the direction of the sun, the front tower looking southwards. The entrance is thus on the side of the building, on Sichuan Zhong Lu. The tower is 15 storeys high, the main body of the building has 10 floors, is terraced and rises towards the tower. The vertical strips between the windows carry on beyond the eaves, going to form a sort of battlement along the top of the building. The windows are small and rectangular, the vertical sides being longer.

JIALING BUILDING

嘉陵大楼

(Liza Hardoon Building)
Date: 1937
Design: P.Tilley, Graham Painter
Function: Offices
Huangpu District
346, Sichuan Zhong Lu
黄浦区四川中路 346 号

21

This villa, just as the Shanghai Grand Theatre designed by the same architect, brought contemporary Western architecture to Shanghai. Showing elements of Rationalist architecture it has a Chinese lay-out looking southward. It is characterized by the assembly and fitting together of pure geometric volumes. The parallelepipeds of the main body, the cylinder form of the stairs to the north, the large practically external cylinder form to the south, the horizontal planes of the terraces and cantilever roofs. Horizontal lines take precedence (cantilever roofs, terraces, tape windows). The northern side of the street is compact and closed-in.

WU'S HOUSE

吴氏住宅

Date: 1935/37
Design:L.E. Hudeck
Function: Offices (Housing)
Jing'an District
333, Tongren Lu
(corner Beijing Lu)
静安区铜仁路 333 号
（北京路路口）

22 GRAND THEATRE

大光明电影院

Date: 1938
Design: L.E. Hudeck
Function: Theatre-Cinema
Huangpu District
216, Nanjing Xi Lu
黄浦区南京西路 216 号

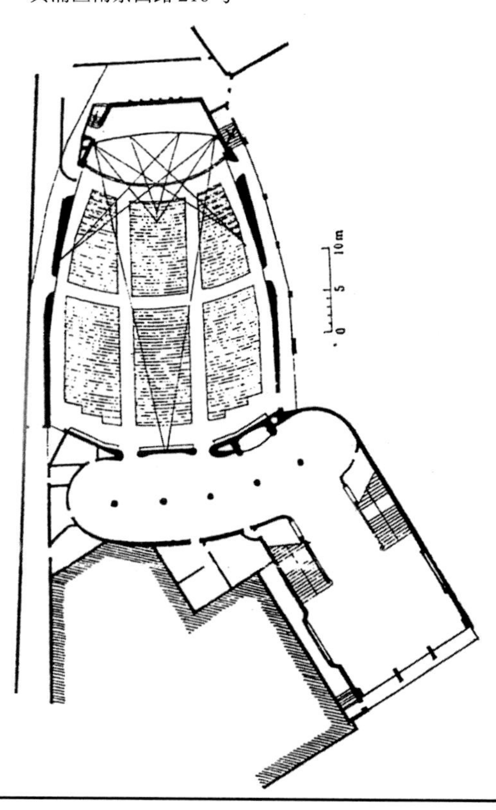

The Shanghai Grand Theatre is an important example of modern architecture in Shanghai. It is a large cinema/theater still in use. The facade is divided into two parts: the long part and the taller foyer section. Between these two zones there is a rectangular tower in milk-white glazing, with nighttime lighting. The facade and all sides of the pyramid-like trunk of the building above the entrance are marked by the contrast offered by emphatic horizontal and vertical lines: overlapping cornices in curved sections are interrupted by thin vertical sections that rise well above the eaves level. The large foyer inside is on two floors, the upper floor accessible from two twin staircases. The original single auditorium, containing stalls and balcony and seating for around 2,400 people, has been divided into two auditoriums on the two floors.

T his is the last building to the south of the twenty-five protected and regulated buildings that form the "building curtain" of the Bund/Waitan. The Swiss/French architect R. Minutti worked mainly in the zone of the former French concession on several residential buildings, including the Savoy Apartment House in Huaihai Zhong Lu and the Hengshan Hotel (Picardie Apartment) in 834, Hengshan Lu (1934), the latter being similar in terms of volume to the Shanghai Mansion and Grosvenor House. The Shanghai Shipping Industrial Co. Building has a very simple shape and is entirely lacking in decoration. Gray concrete plaster was used, the windows are small and rectangular, set in vertical strips, the vertical sides being longer.

SHANGHAI SHIPPING INDUSTRIAL CO. BUILDING

上海船舶工业公司大楼

(法国邮船公司大楼)

(Formerly French Post Office-Compagnie des Maritimes)

Date: 1936

Design: R. Minutti and Co.

Function: Offices

Huangpu District

9, Zhongshan Dong Er Lu

黄浦区中山东二路 9 号

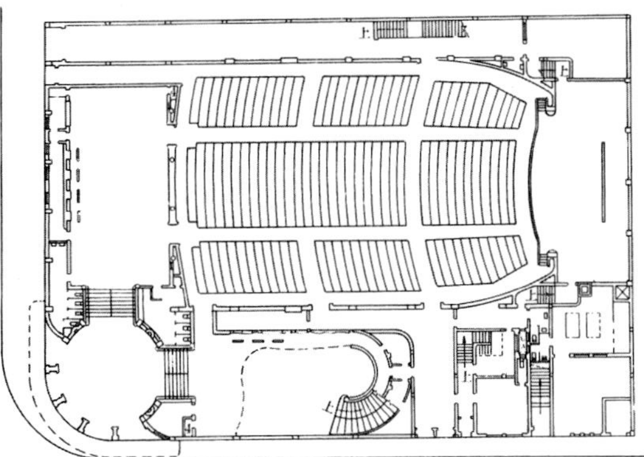

24

MAJESTIC THEATRE

美琪大戏院

Date: 1941

Design: Fan Wenzhao (Robert Fan)

Function: Theatre-Cinema

Jing'an District

66, Jiangning Lu

静安区江宁路 66 号

T he Majestic Theatre, designed by a Chinese architect, brings to mind the form and design of the Paramount Cinema (formerly Paramount Ballroom, Hongdu Theatre) of 1931 (designed by Yang Xiliu) in 218, Yuyuan Lu. The entrance on the corner, pointing southwards, is cylindrical in shape and of twice-normal height inside. The inside foyer develops symmetrically in an L shape in relation to the cylindrical entrance. The auditorium can seat up to 1,600 people (stalls and balcony). The same architect, together with Zhao Shen, designed the Shanghai Music Hall (Nanjing Theatre, 1930) in 523, Yan'an Dong Lu in a neo-classical western style. Another major cinema, the Metropole Theatre (Da Shanghai Cinema) designed by Allied Architects in 500, Xizang Zhong Lu was pulled down in 1997.

Longtang Housing

Itinerary 2

Longtang Housing

Longtang dwellings, a symbol of Shanghai, were the result of an amalgam of Western and Chinese dwelling types. The result is thus a unique architectural style developed in Shanghai by virtue of historical coincidence (economic, social factors, etc.) in the second half of 19th Century. This sort of construction was built till the late 1930s / early 1940s.

Longtang dwellings first emerged within the Foreign Concession zones in Shanghai, initially serving as provisional huts to meet urgent dwelling needs. They are of architectural interest owing to their construction type and transformation from the initial type to the final version. They are of sociological interest by virtue of their considerable use throughout Shanghai, becoming the traditional and most common dwelling type in the city. The first types had to meet Chinese residential needs and at the same time occupy little ground. The first Longtang houses built therefore had both Chinese and Western characteristics, as regards the general urbanistic layout of housing and the typology of the single dwelling unit.

The urbanistic layout brings to mind English terraced housing. Single units are repeated side by side, forming a row of up to ten identical houses. Single rows of houses are placed in parallel fashion one behind the other and oriented so that the front entrance to one row is opposite to the back entrance of another row, with the main rooms and yards pointing southwards (as Chinese tradition). This creates a complex form of main streets leading to alleys (lanes) which in turn lead to single houses. The entire block thus created is closed in on the sides by walls. The degree of airing and wholesomeness of these blocks depends on how wide these internal lanes are and on the presence of trees and shrubs. The layout type is of Chinese tradition by virtue of the hierarchy of spaces and the degree of sharing / privacy of dwellings.

This architectural typology evolved, however, from the original types to later versions: which feature detached houses with courtyard, terraced houses with the yard at the front, terraced houses with garden, small detached houses, apartment buildings built in rows. Changes over the years did not however modify the "serial" nature of these constructions or their southward orientation.

Interest in Longtang housing is due to the integration of styles and the gradual evolution of the typology. It is not so much the decorative elements (cornices, pilaster strips, gables of western taste) that render Longtang houses a blend of Western and Chinese cultures, rather it is their layout typology and evolution.

The new residential districts being built in Shanghai are now completely westernized in terms of single housing units, with buildings in rows consisting of single-family apartments or small detached houses. Modern-day urbanistic layouts are however similar to those of Longtang houses, and thus derive from Chinese tradition. Laid out in closed blocks with few entrances, buildings are aligned and parallel one to the next and one behind the other, with the main rooms on the south side (main facade) and the stairs and utility rooms to the north. Inside the blocks there are kindergartens, green areas and other shared utilities.

The architecture adopted for public residential compounds is extremely simple. In the late 1990s some of these districts have been externally painted and roofed.

The architecture adopted for the new private residential districts in recent years is usually designed by Chinese architects, both mainland and overseas (Taiwan, Japan, HongKong, Singapore) influenced by contemporary and international ideas.

Both Longtang dwellings and new districts are organized in blocks. This means that each block becomes a city within a city, or a small village, where a semi-public environment is created connecting each houses.

The lay-out in both Longtang dwellings and new districts — rows of aligned, same oriented and parallel parallelepipeds oriented southwards — lends to the whole a uniform and monotonous appearance. This lay-out surrounded by an outer wall comes from the Chinese tradition as like as the lay-out of the Forbidden City in Beijing. The perfect symmetrical geometry of the plan of Forbidden City resembles that of a military camp oriented towards the sun (the Emperor was the "child of the sky") and perfectly aligned buildings resemble soldiers lined up for the flag hoisting ceremony.

This itinerary sets out to highlight the development of typologies from the early to the later versions and to show how the typology has gradually evolved from a single dwelling with an internal yard, of Chinese tradition, to buildings in rows. The itinerary is not exactly chronological, but follows progressive changes, which clearly happened over the years.

(There are many other examples of Longtang houses in addition to those described).

Longtang=Li Long
Lane lined and terraced with residential houses

A) Yard Type

The first Longtang houses, two or three floors, were built around a small yard (called "heaven's well") at the front, pointing southwards, onto which the entire dwelling looked. These houses consisted of a main room (the parlour) and side rooms on either side of the yard. At the back of the house was the kitchen, a mezzanine room above the kitchen (Tingzijian), a terrace above this room and a small enclosure for airing. Bedrooms were on the first floor. The front yard was closed in by a high wall separating the house from the internal lane and an important-looking front door (Shikumen). The rooms looking onto the yard had large and tall detachable lattice windows. Sanitary services were not indoor but were shared with neighbors in the lanes. The walls were brickwork, while the floors and staircases were made of wood (to prevent fires the vertical walls extend beyond the pitch of the roof). Such houses were built from the end of the last century up to the 1910s and 1920s and are labeled "Shikumen Houses".

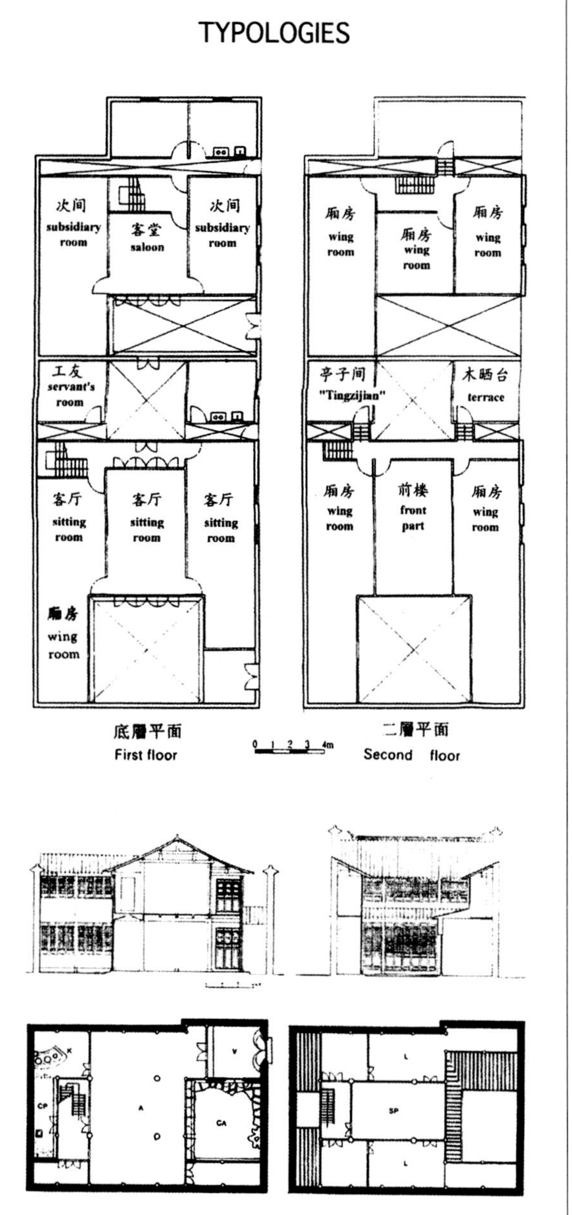

B) Terrace Type

The original type evolved over the years, gradually losing its Chinese elements. The second stage of this process was the loss of the side wings flanking the front yard. In this second period, the yards of different houses are separated only by high walls, which continue to separate only by high walls, (these walls being one storey high). In later periods, these walls were lowered, the front doors began to lose their architectural importance and yards became small gardens separated only by open fences or hedges. This plan is almost always terraced, closed in blocks and aligned on a perfect south / north axis (with the main rooms and facade pointing southwards). These dwellings, built in the 1920s, gradually began to be equipped with water closets and bathrooms.

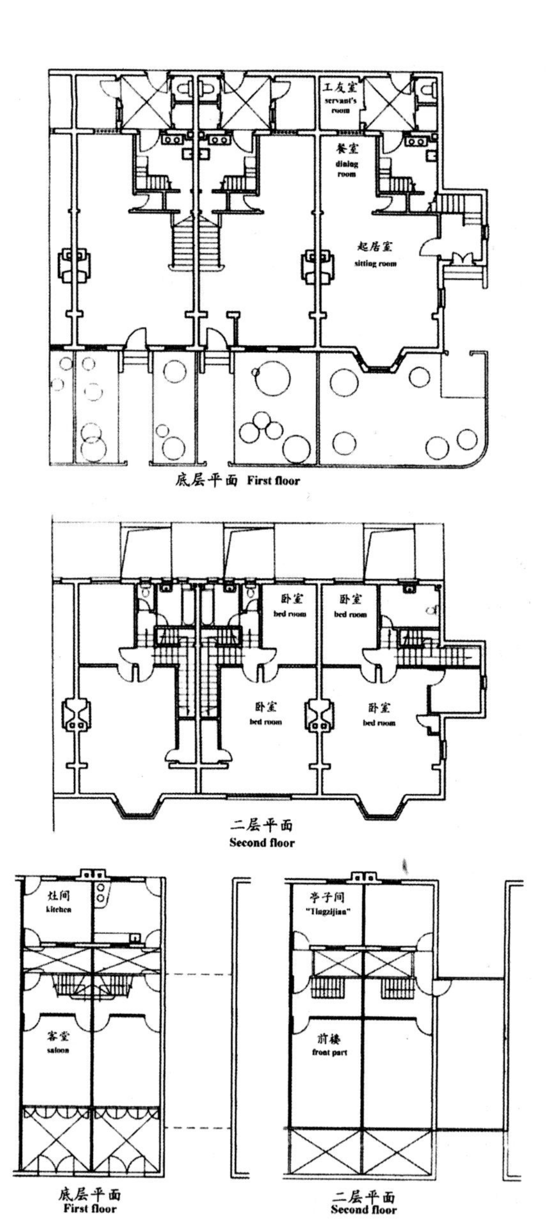

C) Small Detached Houses in Rows

At the same time as the advent of terraced housing in other blocks houses began to become detached, being turned into single-family detached or two-family semi-detached houses. Each house had a large garden to the south, and internal lanes were wider. Some of these houses were divided into apartments, one or two per floor. Higher buildings with four or five storeys for apartments in rows began to appear. These dwellings were equipped with water closets and bathrooms, and were built in brickwork and/or reinforced concrete. In all these cases, in which the construction typology is very different from the initial type, dwellings preserved their block-type urban layout, with two entrances, arrangement in rows and perfect southward alignment. They were built from the end of the 1920s to the beginning of the 1940s.

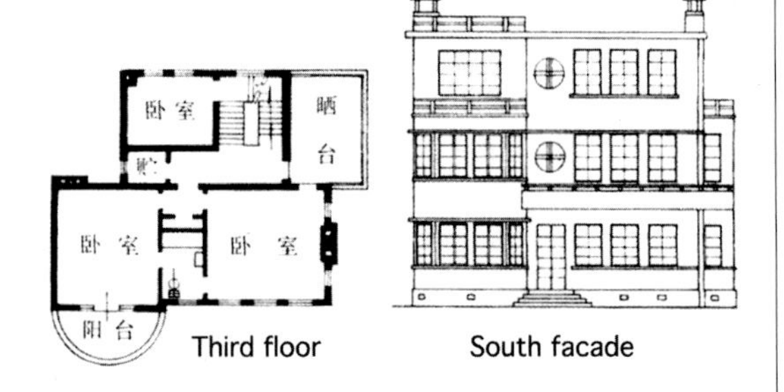

Third floor

South facade

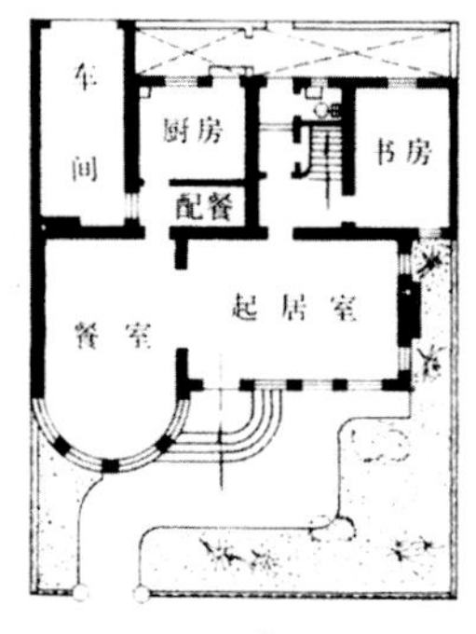

First floor

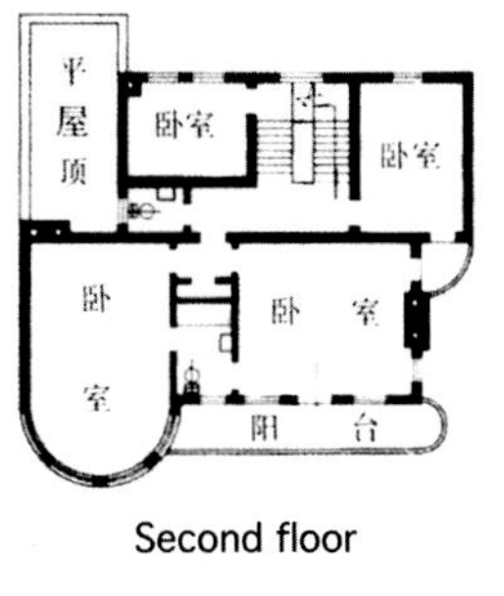

Second floor

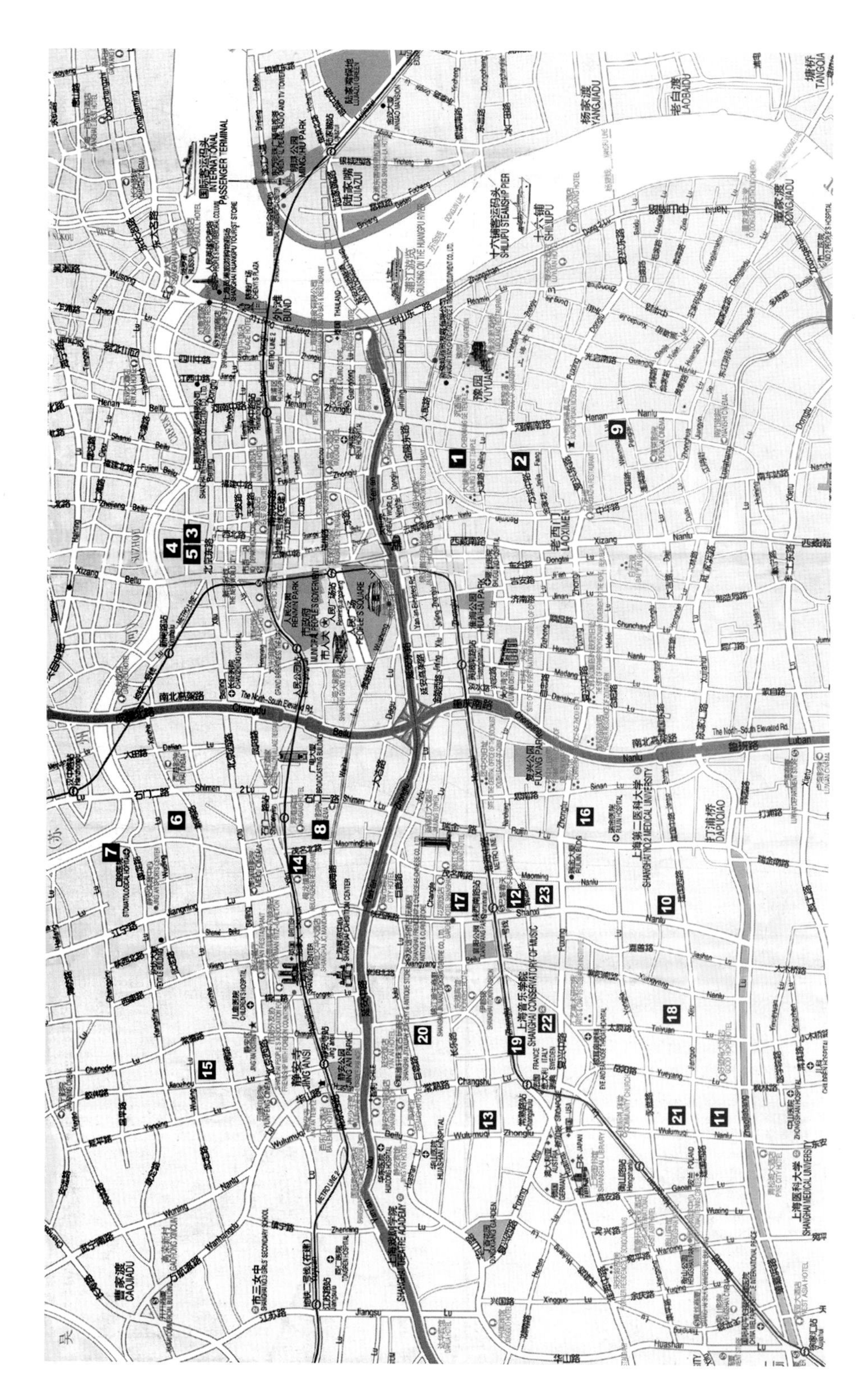

Itinerary 2

HUANGPU(FORMERLY NANSHI)DISTRICT

151/155/157, HOUJIA LU

Type A

南市区侯家路 151,155,157 号

1

Three houses are united in a single block. One with three floors and an internal yard, the other two with two floors and double yard facing the street (but not southwards) separated by a high wall. Black facebricks and recurrences in red bricks.

Two dwellings aligned with the street, facing south. Two floors, single internal yard, rooms along the sides of the yard, high wall separating the yard from the lane and front door with cornice. Black facebricks and recurrences in red bricks. Different architectural details for the two dwellings.

2

HUANGPU(FORMERLY NANSHI)DISTRICT

175/179, JIN JIA FANG LU

Type A

南市区金家坊路 175,179 号

HONG DE LI

Type A
Huangpu District
Lane 756, Beijing Dong Lu
黄浦区北京东路 756 弄

3

This is one of the oldest blocks in existence (1907). The typology is a single yard (with rooms along the sides) or two yards (separated by wall). Very dense urban layout, with internal lanes and narrow side lanes. The architecture is extremely simple, lacking in detail. Plastered walls.

4

Typical example of the earliest type Longtang Shikumen. Single or shared yards. Black facebricks and recurrences in red bricks. Door cornices in gray concrete.

HUANGPU DISTRICT
LANE 136, XIAMEN LU

Type A
黄浦区厦门路 136 弄

BAO KANG LI

保康里

Type A
Huangpu District
Lane 830, Beijing Dong Lu
黄浦区北京东路 830 弄

5

Large block of early Longtang Shikumen type. Single or shared yards, two or three floors. Black facebricks. Great attention to architectural details (cornices of doors and windows, ridge lines).

KANG FU LI

康福里

Type A

Jing'an District

Lane 906, Xinzha Lu

静安区新闸路 906 弄

Large and important block of early Longtang Shikumen type. Single yards, two stories. Outside walls in red facebricks or plaster. Cornices of doors in facebricks. Wider central lane and side lanes.

6

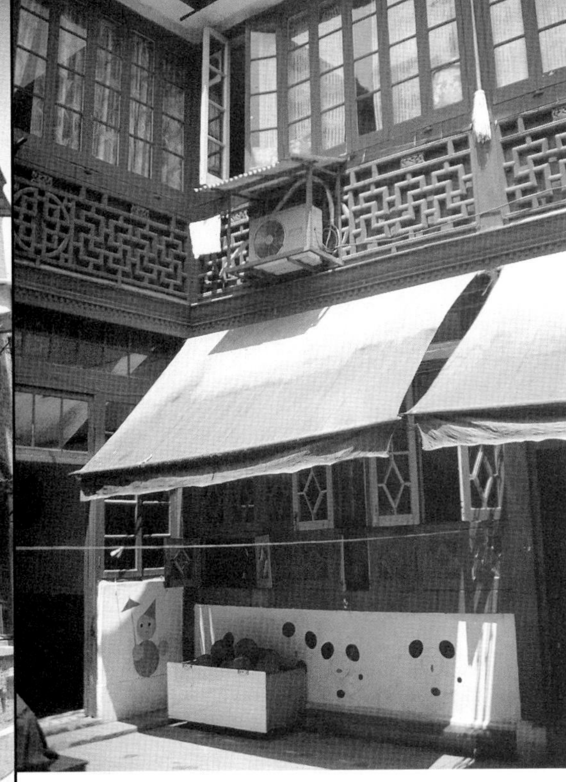

JING'AN DISTRICT

Type A

Lane 481, Taixing Lu

静安区泰兴路 481 弄

7

Large and important block of early Longtang Shikumen type. Single or double yards or terraced type. Two stories. Outside walls in black facebricks and recurrences in red bricks. Great wealth and variety of architectural details: cornices, string-course, ridge lines (in stone or facebricks).

JING'AN DISTRICT

LANE 590-40/56, WEIHAI LU

Type A

静安区威海路590弄40/56号

8

Block of early Shikumen Longtang houses with specific aspects. The lanes separate nine very compact sub-units each taking on the appearance of a fortress, with internal alleys leading to single dwellings. Single yards. Two floors. Outside walls in black facebricks and recurrences in red bricks. Great wealth and variety of architectural details: cornices, string-course, ridge lines (in stone or facebricks).

Shikumen Longtang type renovated in 1980s with internal facilities such as bathroom and kitchen added.

9

SHIKUMEN LONGTANG

里弄住宅

Type A
Lane 303, Penglai Lu
Huangpu District
(formerly Nanshi District)
黄埔区(原南市区)蓬莱路 303 弄
1910s-1920s

CITE BOURGOGNE

步高里

Type A

Jianguo Xi Lu (corner Shaanxi Nan Lu)

Luwan District

卢湾区建国西路(陕西南路路口)

1930s

An important block of Shikumen Longtang type houses. The gates opening to two city roads have strong architectural features.

Terraced block, with yards divided by high walls. Constructed in 1920. Very compact with narrow lanes and side lanes. Two floors plus attic with dormer windows. Plain architectural details. Red facebricks. Protected as part of architectural heritage.

11 JIAN YE LI

建业里

Type B
Xuhui District
Lane 440, Jianguo Xi Lu
徐汇区建国西路440弄

HUAI HAI TERRACE

淮海坊

Type B

Luwan District

Lane 899-927, Huaihai Zhong Lu

卢湾区淮海中路 899-927 弄

12

Large block and typical example of second-type terraced Longtang housing. Year of construction: 1927. Three stories, yard divided by walls (lower wall type). Compact south side with large windows, north split up in terms of volume by the alternation of solid and empty spaces (kitchens and rooms above, enclosures and terraces). Facebricks.

BAO DE LI

褒德里

Type B
Xuhui District
Lane 142, Wuyuan Lu
徐汇区五源路 142 弄

13

Large block and typical example of second-type terraced Longtang housing. Two /three stories, yard divided by walls. Compact south side with large windows, north split up in terms of volume by the alternation of solid and empty spaces (kitchens and rooms above, enclosures and terraces). Facebricks and plaster.

JIANG'AN ESTATE

静安别墅

Type B

Jing'an District

Lane 1025, Nanjing Xi Lu

静安区南京西路 1025 弄

14

Large block and typical example of second-type terraced Longtang housing. Three stories, yard (garden type) divided by walls (lower wall type). Western renaissance-like architectural details (balconies with columns and spiral corbels, Serlian-type windows). Facebricks. Protected as part of architectural heritage.

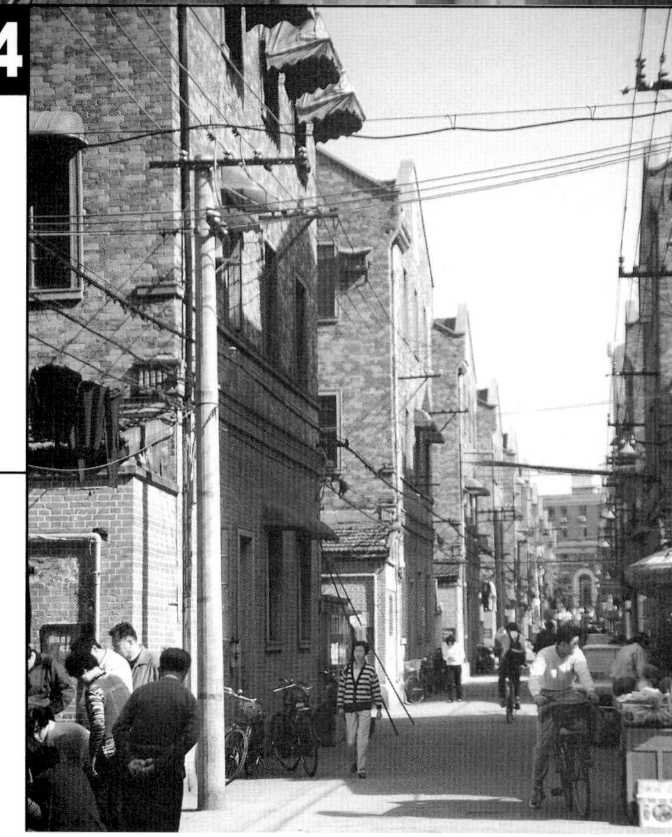

Terraced housing with small garden divided by fencing. The rows of buildings are not linked by a central lane but a city street. Two stories. Architectural style: Spanish-Mediterranean

15

RUI ZHI TERRACE

瑞之村

Type B

Jing'an District

Lane 148, Jiaozhou Lu

静安区胶州路 148 弄

16

Block containing different typologies: terraced, small detached,apartments. Three and five floors. Dwellings are not all oriented southwards. Facebricks, pitch roofs and wooden rafters below the pitch.

FU XING TERRACE

复兴坊

Type B

Type C

Luwan District

Lane 553, Fuxing Zhong Lu

卢湾区复兴中路 553 弄

17

Typical terraced housing with small front garden. Year of construction: 1925. Their classification in the Longtang typology is due to their being united in a single block and to their perfect southward orientation. Two stories. Architectural style: European Alpine. Protected as part of architectural heritage.

VERDUN GARDEN

凡尔登花园

Type B

Type C

Luwan District

Lane 39, Shaanxi Nan Lu

卢湾区陕西南路 39 弄

Large block consisting of terraced housing (two stories), semi-detached houses (two floors) in rows and a three-story apartment building. Perfect southward alignment and orientation. Extensive green areas. Architectural style: Spanish Mediterranean.

TAI YUAN TERRACE

太原新村

Type B

Type C

Xuhui District

Lane 45, Taiyuan Lu

徐汇区太原路 45 弄

19

Block consisting of small detached houses (three stories) in a row. Year of construction: 1938/39. Perfect southward alignment and orientation. Extensive green areas. Two architectural styles: Spanish Mediterranean and Rationalist.

SHANG FANG GARDEN

上方花园

Type C

Xuhui District

Lane 1285, Huaihai Zhong Lu

徐汇区淮海中路 1285 弄

YU HUA TERRACE
玉华新村

Type C
Jing'an District
Lane 182, Fumin Lu
静安区富民路 182 弄

20

Block of three-story semi-detached and terraced houses. In terms of volume, similar to the blocks in Lane 142, Wuyuan Lu and Lane 927 Huaihai Zhong Lu: compact south face, division of northern face, visible chimneys. Wright-style architecture.

Large block consisting of two parts. One part has three-story buildings in a row, with four apartments per floor: very simple architecture. The second part consists of two-story semi-detached houses, with small front garden: Spanish/Chinese architectural style. Year of construction: 1936.

21

YONG JIA TERRACE

永嘉新村

Type B

Type C

Xuhui District

Lane 580, Yongjia Lu

徐汇区永嘉路 580 弄

Block consisting of two parts along an extensive central lane. One part consisting of four five-story buildings in a row. Second part with eleven two-story small detached houses with large front garden. Architectural style: Spanish Mediterranean for detached houses and Rationalist for the high-rise buildings. Year of construction: 1933/34.

22

XIN KANG GARDEN

新康花园

Type C

Xuhui District

Lane 1360, Fuxing Zhong Lu/

Lane 1273, Huaihai Zhong Lu

徐汇区复兴中路 1360 弄

淮海中路 1273 弄

SHAAN NAN VILLAGE
陕南村

Type C
Luwan District
Lane 185, Shaanxi Nan Lu
卢湾区陕西南路 185 弄

23

Block consisting of sixteen four-story buildings in rows, with four apartments per floor. Green areas. Jutting pitch roofs, alternation of bricks and peel-effect plaster, polygonal bow windows in corners, chimneys visible. Period of construction: late 1920.

Wall's

Itinerary 3

Palmer & Turner Architecture and the Bund/Waitan

Palmer & Turner Studio designed Shanghai's most important public buildings in the 1920s and 1930s and some of the new skyscrapers in the 1990s. The importance of this studio for the city is thus mainly due to the quantity and importance of buildings that it has designed and built: the image of Shanghai itself is marked by Palmer & Turner's major works.

In the 1920s and 1930s, the studio designed the seat of the Bank of China and of the Hong Kong and Shanghai Banking Corporation, Customs House, Sassoon House and other buildings in the Bund/Waitan waterfront area. Other important buildings of those years, including hotels and residential buildings such as Grosvenor House, the Embankment Building, Hamilton House and the Metropole Hotel, continue to represent Shanghai's urban and architectural layout.

In the 1990s, the studio continued to be active under the same name, in Hong Kong (where its founders came from) and Singapore. After sixty years' absence from the city, it has returned to Shanghai to design and build new skyscrapers, no longer of primary importance in terms of position and function but still of considerable significance for the city's image.

Architectural choices made in the 1920s, 1930s and 1990s were usually closely tied up with international (Western) stylistic trends of the periods in question, without being particularly original or theoretically demanding. The only works of interest are probably those that attempt to unite local Chinese tradition with imported Western languages. As far as the 1930s in particular is concerned, the central seat of the Bank of China and the small former R.A.S. building are two examples of the integration between Chinese and Western architecture. As regards the 1990s, the Harbour Ring Plaza skyscraper may be regarded as international style architecture but its urban positioning falls into line with Chinese tradition.

There can therefore be no doubts as to the importance of the Palmer & Turner Studio played in the construction of the skyline of Shanghai. Our interest is chiefly due to the first historical attempts it made to blend Western architecture with Chinese architecture and tastes, and to the different city-planning choices made in the early decades of the 20th century as compared with the 1990s.

In the 1920s and 1930s, in foreign concessions, buildings respected the city's urban plan or went to determine the plan according to Western tradition, such as the Bund/Waitan riverside area and the Hamilton House crossroads.

In the 1990s, on the other hand, skyscrapers, and the Harbour Ring Plaza in particular, the great city landmark in the main square, appear to respect the Chinese tradition of orienting buildings southwards.

The Bund/Waitan: A Western Urban Space

The Bund/Waitan is the waterfront area and the symbol of historic Shanghai. About twenty-five buildings stand one after another along the left side of Huangpu River from the Suzhou Creek toward south in a homogeneous waterfront. The existing buildings are built in the period from the last years of 19th Century — the Imperial Bank of China Building, the Dali Building, the South Wing of Peace Hotel — to the year 1936 — the Bank of China Building. All of these are now preserved under law.

The waterfront represents the Western city concepts in Shanghai. Together with other important buildings in the Huangpu District — the Hamilton crossroads and the north side of People's Square (the former Hippodrome). this part of Huangpu District — between the Bund/Waitan and the People's Square — contains the most markedly urban features of a Western kind, with the buildings ranged along the street and conferring an identity on it as an open space. The Hamilton crossroads — with the four arched structures set back from the street to create an urban space in the center — is another significant city-planning solution adopted in the city.

The building curtain along the Bund/Waitan, constructed during the foreign concession period, follows the natural loop of the river, creating an urban space and architectural backdrop like a Western city. The building curtain and the natural flow of the river compensate each other in creating a picturesque city scene. As a background perspective for the Bund/Waitan, the Shanghai Mansion is one of the few buildings in Shanghai of urbanistic importance.

This layout and planning gives this setting the sense of a spatial basin defined by the relationship between constructions and the emptiness around or – in this case — in front of them; as like as the Western streets, waterfronts, park-crescent tradition is.

Such kind of city planning has no relation with the Chinese tradition. In Shanghai the two different city concepts — Western and Chinese - are clear and evident: the Bund/Waitan represents the former while the latter is represented by the new People's Square . In Chinese tradition there is no such thing as a "facade" and the streets are thus not an architectural backdrop. Perspective constructions do not exists at all, too.

The Western style of all these twenty-five buildings alone does not make up the Western city concepts. The Western ideas of city planning and the consequential lay-out together with the Western style buildings make the Bund/Waitan a Western urban space. The Bund/Waitan was built during the foreign concession period in the International Settlement by English or other Western owners and designed by their architects.

1920s and 1930s

1. SHANGHAI ARCHITECTURAL DESIGN INSTITUTE

上海市建筑设计研究院
17, Guangdong Lu
Huangpu District
黄浦区广东路 17 号
1916 - Offices

2. HUALIAN COMMERCIAL BUILDING

华联商厦
635, Nanjing Dong Lu
Huangpu District
黄浦区南京东路 635 号
1918 - Department Store

3. YANGZI BUILDING

扬子大楼
26, Zhongshan Dong Yi Lu
Huangpu District (Bund/Waitan)
中山东一路 26 号
黄浦区（外滩）
1920 - Offices

4. SHANGHAI CULTURE AND BROADCASTING TV BUREAU

上海文化广播影视管理局
2, Beijing Dong Lu
Huangpu District (Bund/Waitan)
北京东路 2 号
黄浦区（外滩）
1921- Offices

5.CHUNJIANG BUILDING

春江大楼
18, Zhongshan Dong Yi Lu
Huangpu District (Bund/Waitan)
中山东一路 18 号
黄浦区（外滩）
1923- Offices

6.SHANGHAI PUDONG DEVELOPMENT BANK

上海浦东发展银行
（原上海市人民政府，汇丰银行）
10-12, Zhongshan Dong Yi Lu
Huangpu District (Bund/Waitan)
中山东一路 10-12 号
黄浦区（外滩）
1923- Offices

7. INDUSTRIAL AND COMMERCIAL BANK OF CHINA, BUND BRANCH

Formerly Yokohama Specie Bank
中国工商银行外滩支行
（原日本横滨正金银行，上海分行）
24, Zhongshan Dong Yi Lu
Huangpu District (Bund/Waitan)
中山东一路 24 号
黄浦区（外滩）
1924- Offices

8.CUSTOM HOUSE

上海海关大楼
13, Zhongshan Dong Yi Lu
Huangpu District (Bund/Waitan)
中山东一路 13 号
黄浦区（外滩）
1927- Offices

9.PEACE HOTEL

Formerly Sassoon House, Cathy Hotel
和平饭店北楼
（原沙逊大厦，华懋饭店）
20, Nanjing Dong Lu
Huangpu District (Bund/Waitan)
南京东路 20 号
黄浦区（外滩）
1926/28- Hotel

10. CHINA MERCHANTS BANK SHANGHAI BRANCH

招商银行上海分行

16, Zhongshan Dong Yi Lu
Huangpu District (Bund/Waitan)
中山东一路 16 号
黄浦区(外滩)
1931- offices

11. CYPRESS HOTEL, BUILDING NO. 1

龙柏饭店一号楼

2419, Hongqiao Lu
Changning District
长宁区虹桥路 2419 号
1932-Hotel

12.FORMER R.A.S. BUILDING

(Royal Asiatic Society)

原亚洲文会北中国支会会址

20, Huqiu Lu
Huangpu District
黄浦区虎丘路 20 号
1932- Offices

13.FUZHOU BUILDING

Formerly Hamilton House

福州大楼（原汉弥登大楼）

170, Jiangxi Zhong Lu
Huangpu District
黄浦区江西中路 170 号
1931/33- Hotel

14.HEBING DALOU

Formerly Embankment Building

河滨大楼

310-434, Bei Suzhou Lu
Hongkou District
虹口区北苏州路 310-434 号
1931/35- Housing

15. PEOPLE'S CONSTRUCTION BANK OF CHINA, SHANGHAI BRANCH

中国人民建设银行，上海分行

50, Jiujiang Lu
Huangpu District
黄浦区九江路 50 号
1934- Offices

16.XINCHENG HOTEL

Formerly Metropole Hotel

新城饭店

180, Jiangxi Zhong Lu
Huangpu District
黄浦区江西中路 180 号
1934- Hotel

17. JINJIANG HOTEL, MIDDLE BUILDING

Formerly Grosvenor House

锦江饭店北楼

87, Maoming Nan Lu
Luwan District
卢湾区茂名南路 87 号
1935- Hotel

18.THE BANK OF CHINA

中国银行大楼

23, Zhongshan Dong Yi Lu
Huangpu District (Bund/Waitan)
中山东一路 23 号
黄浦区(外滩)
1936/37- Offices
Architect: Lu Qianshou (H.S.Luke)

Itinerary 3

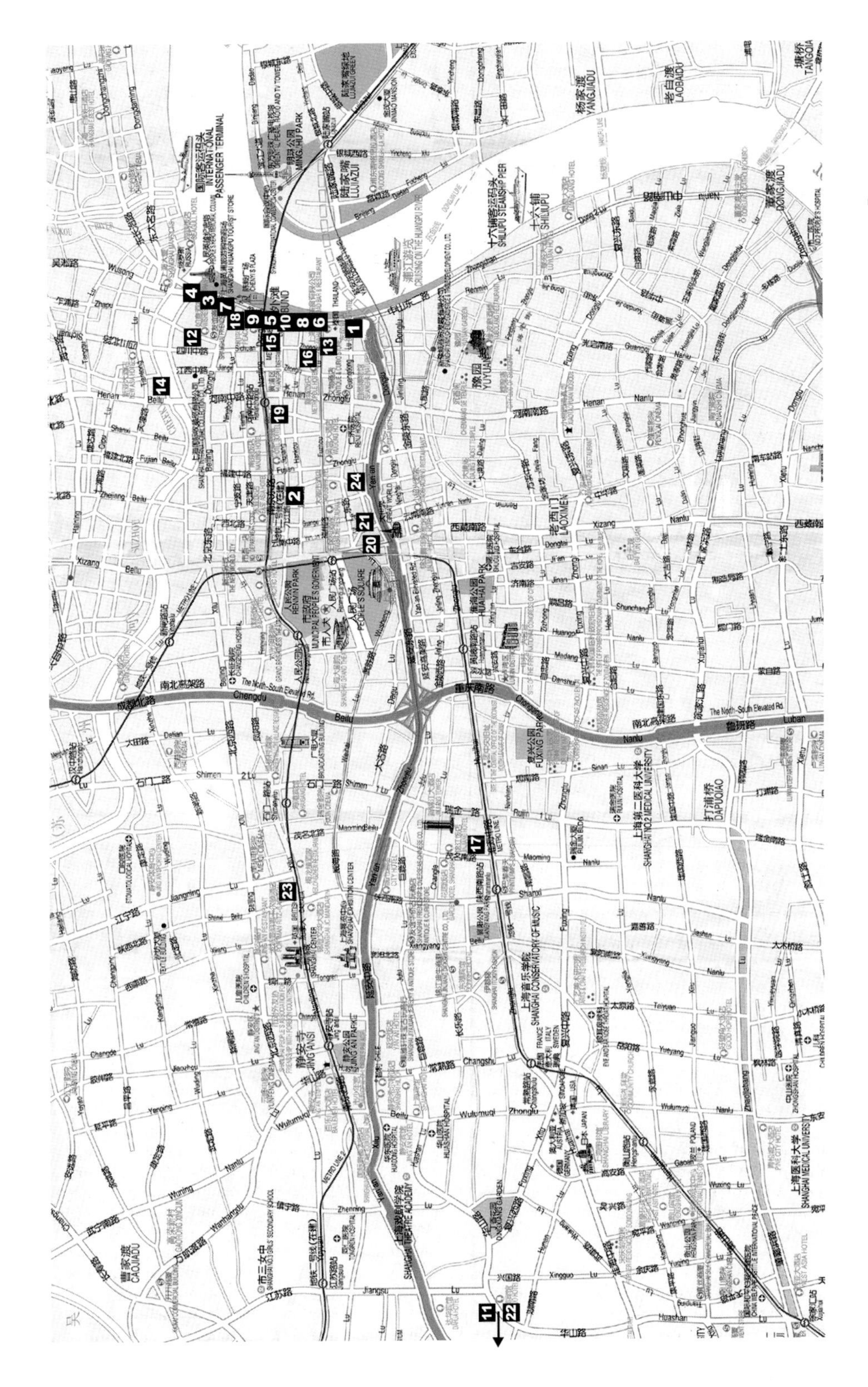

In the 1990s

19 SHANGHAI LANDMARK ▼

上海置地广场

Nanjing Dong Lu (corner Shanxi Nan Lu)
Huangpu District
黄浦区南京东路（山西南路路口）
1997- Offices, Shopping mall
Architects: Palmer & Turner, Singapore + ECADI, Shanghai

20 ▲ HARBOUR RING PLAZA

港陆广场

Yan'an Dong Lu (corner Xizang Zhong Lu)
Huangpu District
黄浦区延安东路（西藏中路路口）
1998- Offices

21 ▲ EAST OCEAN CENTRE

东海商业中心

Yan'an Dong Lu (corner Yunnan Zhong Lu)
Huangpu District
黄浦区延安东路（云南中路路口）
1998- Offices

22

◀ PACIFIC CENTRE

太平洋企业中心

Jiangsu Lu (corner Yan'an Xi Lu)
Changning District
长宁区江苏路（延安西路路口）

1998- Offices

23

◀▲ CITIC SQUARE

中信泰富广场

Nanjing Xi Lu (corner Jiangning Lu)
Jing'an District
静安区南京西路（江宁路路口）
2000- Offices, Shopping mall

24

OCEAN TOWERS

海塔

Yan'an Dong Lu (corner Fujian Zhong Lu)
Huangpu District
黄浦区延安东路（福建中路路口）
Under construction - Offices

(consultants with ECADI, Shanghai)

▲ Bund/Waitan from south

Bund/Waitan in 1920s ▶

Buildings on Bund/Waitan Waterfront (from north to south)

A) SHANGHAI MANSION
(ITINERARY 1 – 14)
Date: 1934

B) FORMER BANQUE DE L'INDO-CHINE
Date: 1911
Design: Atkinson&Dallas

C) SHANGHAI CULTURE AND BROADCASTING TV BUREAU
(ITINERARY 3 – 4)
DATE: 1921 **DESIGN:** Palmer&Turner

D) FOREIGN TRADE BLDG.
DATE: 1922 **DESIGN:** Stewardson&Spence

E) YANGZI BLDG.
(ITINERARY 3 – 3)
DATE: 1920 **DESIGN:** Palmer&Turner

F) INDUSTRIAL AND COMMERCIAL BANK OF CHINA
(ITINERARY 3 – 7)
DATE: 1924 **DESIGN:** Palmer&Turner

G) BANK OF CHINA
(ITINERARY 3 – 18 AND 1 – 19)
DATE: 1936/37 **DESIGN:** Palmer&Turner

H) PEACE HOTEL
(ITINERARY 3 – 9 AND 1 – 2)
DATE: 1926/28 **DESIGN:** Palmer&Turner

I) PEACE HOTEL, SOUTH BUILDING
DATE: 1906 **DESIGN:** W. Scott

J) CHUNJIANG BLDG.
(ITINERARY 3 – 5)
DATE: 1923 **DESIGN:** Palmer&Turner

K) GUILIN BLDG.
DATE: 1924 **DESIGN:** Lester, Johnson and Morris

L) CHINA MERCHANTS BANK SHANGHAI BRANCH
(ITINERARY 3 – 10)
DATE: 1931 **DESIGN:** Palmer&Turner

M) CHINA FOREIGN EXCHANGE CENTRE
DATE: 1901 **DESIGN:** H. Becker

N) SHANGHAI GENERAL TRADE UNION
DATE: 1947 **DESIGN:** C.H. Gonda

O) CUSTOM HOUSE
(ITINERARY 3 – 8)
DATE: 1927 **DESIGN:** Palmer&Turner

P) SHANGHAI PUDONG DEVELOPMENT BANK
(ITINERARY 3 – 6 AND 4 – 1B)
DATE: 1923 **DESIGN:** Palmer&Turner

Q) DALI BUILDING
DATE: 1901 **DESIGN**: Atkinson&Dallas

R) FORMER GREAT NORTHERN TELEGRAPH CORP.
DATE: 1906 **DESIGN:** Atkinson&Dallas

S) FORMER IMPERIAL BANK OF CHINA
DATE: 1897 **DESIGN:** G.J. Morrison and F.M. Gratton

T) FORMER NISHIN NAVIGATION COMPANY
DATE: 1921 **DESIGN:** Lester, Johnson and Morris

U) FORMER UNION BUILDING
(ITINERARY 3 – 1)
DATE: 1916 **DESIGN:** Palmer&Turner

V) DONG FENG HOTEL(FORMERLY SHANGHAI CLUB)
DATE: 1911 **DESIGN:** Moorhead and Halse

W) FORMER ASIA PETROLEUM COMPANY BUILDING
DATE: 1916 **DESIGN:** Moorhead and Halse

X) SHANGHAI SHIPPING INDUSTRIAL CORPORATION BUILDING (ITINERARY 1-23)
DATE: 1936 **DESIGN:** R. Minutti

Q) DALI BUILDING ►
DATE: 1901
DESIGN: Atkinson&Dallas

◄ R) FORMER GREAT NORTHERN TELEGRAPH CORP.
DATE: 1906
DESIGN: Atkinson&Dallas

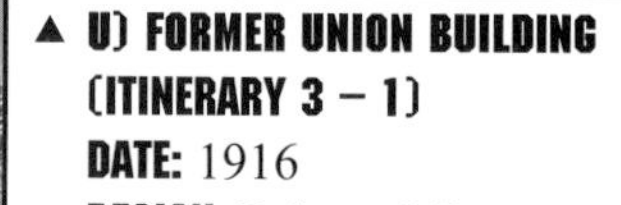

▲ U) FORMER UNION BUILDING (ITINERARY 3 – 1)
DATE: 1916
DESIGN: Palmer&Turner

◄ V) DONG FENG HOTEL
DATE: 1911
DESIGN: Moorhead and Halse

▼ W) FORMER ASIA PETROLEUM COMPANY BUILDING
DATE: 1916
DESIGN: Moorhead and Halse

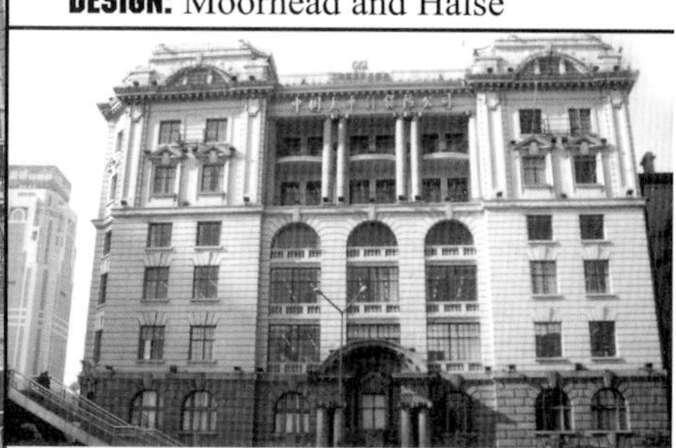

▲ **D) FOREIGN TRADE BLDG.**
DATE: 1922
DESIGN: Stewardson& Spence

▶ **O) CUSTOM HOUSE (ITINERARY 3 – 8)**
DATE: 1927
DESIGN: Palmer&Turner

◀ **I) PEACE HOTEL, SOUTH BUILDING**
DATE: 1906
DESIGN: W. Scott

▶ **M) CHINA FOREIGN EXCHANGE CENTRE**
DATE: 1901
DESIGN: H. Becker

Itinerary 4

Shanghai in the 1990s

Since the later 1980s and the early 1990s, Shanghai has grown enormously and changed radically. In the city center and neighboring districts, huge areas are being pulled down to make more intense use of the land. Areas containing old and very poorly kept low buildings (suffering from overcrowding, lack of maintenance, poor construction quality) are making way for new high-rise multipurpose buildings (offices, housing, hotels, shopping centres, etc.). The new elevated roadways being built are another reason for the demolition of existing buildings. There are also some new development areas in the semi-central suburbs: Hongqiao Development Zone for international trade, Pudong Financial Area and other industrially important zones.

This huge transformation means great and fast construction activity: intense building work, great linguistic and stylistic variety. People are more enthusiastic in putting up buildings of various kinds and not enough attention has been paid to overall and long-term city planning. Skyscrapers appear here and there in the city. No common language is employed by builders. There are no great city parks. This points to a city in which city planning is in the hands of capital and not city planners. Hundreds of millions of dollars of financial backing are indeed needed to act. The fast construction activity means also a lack of architectural clarity and even the absence of solutions to purely building-related problems. At the same time, however, this situation also permits considerable freedom of language and new architectural images, in short: new architectural frontiers.

Many different architectural styles are evident, following an infinite number of architectural trends: Western style in general but also local style: modern, historical, regional and international styles.

The most interesting note is the blend of these languages and above all the integration of Western and traditional Chinese styles. This makes Shanghai a sort of test bed for international architecture activity regarding the meeting/clash of Western and Chinese architectural cultures.

In amongst so many different solutions there are some common ideas: an open-minded use of architecture rules, building materials, geometric volumes, and an indifference to the urban context. This means great variety, great confusion, and also possibly new ideas.

All these activities may not yet provide innovative impetus for other parts of the world. Such stylistic variety could mark — or not — the beginning of new architectural ideas.

In this scenario — just as in the past — the meeting in Shanghai of China and the West has produced unexpected and surprising results. This clash is the city's foremost feature. On the other hand, property speculation, Chinese taste, old and modern Western colonialism are not the most interesting and by no means the most innovative aspects of this architecture.

In Shanghai today there are almost all the architectural ideas and city concepts of the last century and even before, both Western and Chinese. In the same area many different styles and city concepts overlap one another. Sometimes blended, sometimes clashing. Nothing is more evident or important than other: nor a historical period or an architectural style. The contemporary public buildings, such as the Oriental Pearl TV Tower, the People's Square, the Jinmao Building, are the new symbols of Shanghai: the historical heritage is not anymore the core of the city.

There is the old Chinese traditional architecture and the modern reconstruction in traditional style, as the Market area in the Old City and the Longhua New Town.

The new modern Chinese architecture is in the main public buildings such as in the People's Square, the Municipal Library and the buildings by the architecture institutes of Shanghai, like the three Broadcasting Buildings, the Hongqiao Area and many others in Pudong New Area and among the city.

The socialistic architecture is in the residential housing compounds and other public institutions like hospitals, universities and schools, from the 1950s to the mid 1990s.

In terms of Western city concepts there are the following points. The three/four/five levels of highways, railways and pedestrian overpasses resemble the drawings by the Italian Futurist architect Antonio Sant'Elia in 1920s. The highway "spaghetti" junctions with new trees in middle recall the European architect L. Krier's drawings in the 1980s. The open-air pedestrian shopping areas in Nanjing Lu, Xintiandi Area and other smaller areas are similar to the historical pedestrian streets in the European cities. In Pudong the combination between skyscrapers and the waterfront expressly recalls Manhattan island in New York. In Hongqiao the combination between skyscrapers, elevated highway, park and artificial lake is modeled after North-American cities and the LeCourbusier's city new concepts. The Science City in Pudong resembles the new areas in Paris such as Defense and Tres Grand Bibliotheque.

In terms of Western architectural ideas there are the following points. The Bund resembles the financial City District in London. The Shanghai Grand Theatre and the Circus World recall LeCourbusier's architecture. The International Style is in the most numerous quantity of high-rise buildings: the most representative are the works by Palmer&Turner Studio. The Post Modern architecture is in the Gee House and many other residential and office buildings among the city. The new British ideas for high-tech buildings is realized in the Jiushi Tower by Norman Foster. The "engineering esthetic" of huge buildings is in the Pudong Airport, similar to all other recent airports all over the world. The KPF's buildings — the Finance Center and the Plaza 66 — represent the high quality contemporary international architecture, worldwide from USA to Europe, from South America to Sydney or Shanghai.

The mixture of Western and Chinese architecture is the most interesting. This is the new frontier of architecture where Shanghai is the main and historical playground.

The collaboration between foreign architects and the architectural institutes of Shanghai — although not always with positive results — has many and important examples: combining Western ideas and technologies with Chinese traditional architecture. Such as the Shanghai Centre in the 1980s by John Portman, USA and ECADI, Shanghai; the Jinmao Building by SOM, USA and ECADI, Shanghai; the Shanghai Grand Theatre by ARTE-Charpentier Studio, France and ECADI, Shanghai.

Two buildings in particular are worth mentioning in this context, examples of this new trend: the Jinmao Building and the Shanghai Grand Theatre. The Jinmao Building is a skyscraper with an architectural style that conjures up the style of Chinese pagodas through the use of overlapping roofs. The Shanghai Grand Theatre is different in nature, the horizontal axis being predominant. Its key feature is the large curved roof, concave skywards, suspended and almost detached from the body below. Here there is an even more symbolic reference to the traditional Chinese building.

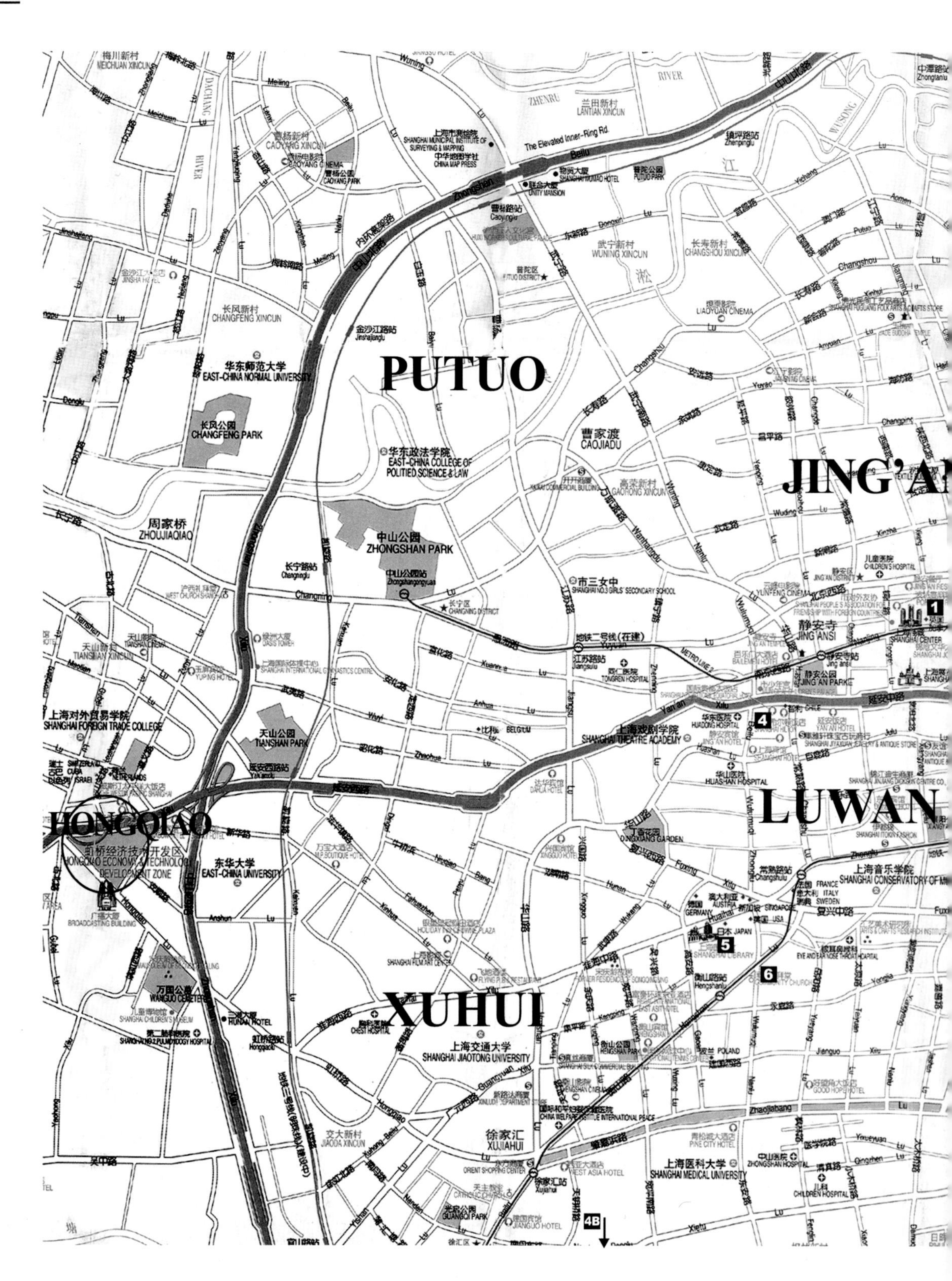
PUTUO
JING'AN
LUWAN
XUHUI
HONGQIAO
长风公园
CHANGFENG PARK
华东师范大学
EAST-CHINA NORMAL UNIVERSITY
中山公园
ZHONGSHAN PARK
天山公园
TIANSHAN PARK
曹家渡
CAOJIADU
周家桥
ZHOUJIAQIAO
虹桥经济技术开发区
HONGQIAO ECONOMIC & TECHNOLOGY DEVELOPMENT ZONE
东华大学
EAST-CHINA UNIVERSITY
上海对外贸易学院
SHANGHAI FOREIGN TRADE COLLEGE
上海戏剧学院
SHANGHAI THEATRE ACADEMY
上海交通大学
SHANGHAI JIAOTONG UNIVERSITY
徐家汇
XUJIAHUI
上海医科大学
SHANGHAI MEDICAL UNIVERSITY
上海音乐学院
SHANGHAI CONSERVATORY OF M
静安寺
JING'ANSI
万国公墓
WANGUO CEMETERY
丁香花园
DINGXIANG GARDEN
The Elevated Inner-Ring Rd.

HONGKOU
HUANGPU
PUDONG
(NANSHI)
RAILWAY STATION
INTERNATIONAL
PASSENGER TERMINAL
国际客运码头
外滩
BUND
人民公园
RENMIN PARK
人民广场
PEOPLE'S SQUARE
陆家嘴
LUJIAZUI
明珠公园
MINGZHU PARK
豫园
YUYUAN
老西门
LAOXIMEN
十六铺
SHILIUPU
十六铺客运码头
SHILIUPU STEAMSHIP PIER
浦江游览
CRUISING ON THE HUANGPU RIVER
杨家渡
YANGJIADU
老白渡
LAOBAIDU
董家渡
DONGJIADU
塘桥
TANGQIAO
提篮桥
TILANQIAO
复兴公园
FUXING PARK
淮海公园
HUAIHAI PARK
金茂大厦
JINMAO MANSION
和平公园
HEPING
River
3
7
8
9
10
11
13
14
15
16
17
18
1B
2B
3B
5B
6B

Itinerary 4

A) New Buildings

SHANGHAI PORTMAN CENTRE

上海商城

1376, Nanjing Xi Lu
Jing'an District
静安区南京西路 1376 号
Date: Completed at the end of 1980s
Design: J. PORTMAN ASS.(USA)+ ECADI (Shanghai)
Function: Hotel, Office, Residential, Theatre

1

Three skyscrapers and one theatre in a traditional Chinese layout: tallest of the three buildings in the centre, set back, other two to the left and right, courtyard in the middle looking south.

GARDEN HOTEL+LOBBY

(lobby formerly the French Sports Club)

花园饭店

(原法国总会)
Maoming Nan Lu
(between Changle Lu and Huaihai Lu)
Luwan District
卢湾区茂名南路
(长乐路和淮海路之间)
Date: Completed at the end of 1980s
Design: OBAYASHI Corp. (Japan)+ECADI (Shanghai)
Function: Hotel

2

Parallelepiped skyscraper with facade facing south, aligned in the same way as the former French Sports Club House (by A.Leonard and P.Veysseyre, 1924) restored during the new construction and now the hotel lobby.

BROADCASTING AND TV BUILDING

上海广播电视国际新闻交流中心

Nanjing Xi Lu
(between Shimen Yi Lu and Chengdu Bei Lu)
Jing'an District
静安区南京西路(石门一路和成都北路之间)
Date: Completed early 1990s
Design: ECADI (Shanghai)
Function: Office, Entertainment

3

Tower in triangular plan, three big cylinders at the corners of triangle. See also the Shanghai TV Station Building in Jing'an District and Shanghai Broadcasting Building in Changning District by the same Institute in the same years.

OVERSEAS CHINESE BUILDING

上海华侨大厦

Yan'an Xi Lu
(corner Wulumuqi Bei Lu)
Jing'an District
静安区延安西路(乌鲁木齐北路路口)
Date: Completed 1996
Design: PEI-KENG, A. PENG
(HongKong-Canada)
Function: Office

4

Tower in triangular plan, three large cylinder sections at the corner of triangle; the iron lattice beam on the top expressly recalls the first iron bridge over the Suzhou Creek. Cylindrical reinforced pillars recall traditional Chinese wooden joints.

5

SHANGHAI MUNICIPAL LIBRARY

上海图书馆

Huaihai Zhong Lu (corner Gaoan Lu)
Xuhui District
徐汇区淮海中路(高安路路口)
Date: Completed 1997
Design: Shanghai Architectural Design Institute
Function: Library Building

Example of contemporary Chinese architecture, facing the main street according to the Western tradition. Two twin towers, one taller and bigger, with pyramid tops. Monumental entrance in centre.

6

GEE HOUSE

芝大厦及芝明俱乐部

41, Hengshan Lu
(corner Wulumuqi Nan Lu)
Xuhui District
徐汇区衡山路41号
(乌鲁木齐南路路口)
Date: Completed 1998
Design: P.FUNG Ass.
(Hong Kong)+ECADI(Shanghai)
Function: Residential Apartment

Large building with symmetrical layout and curved facade in European style. Post-modern architecture.

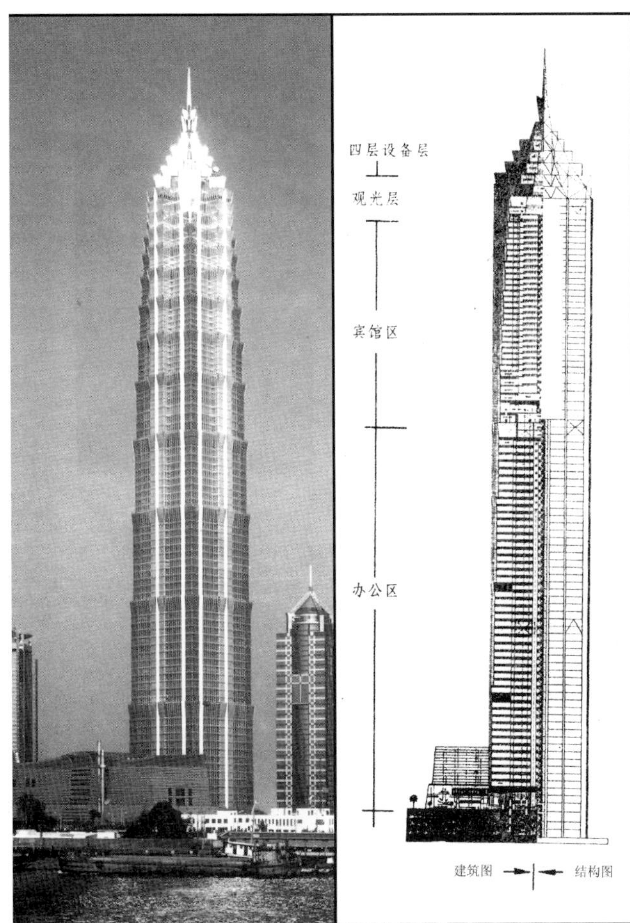

7

JINMAO TOWER

金茂大厦

88 Century Boulevard, Pudong

浦东世纪大道 88 号

Date: Completed 1998

Design: SOM (USA)+ECADI(Shanghai)

Function: Office, Hotel, Congress and Entertainment

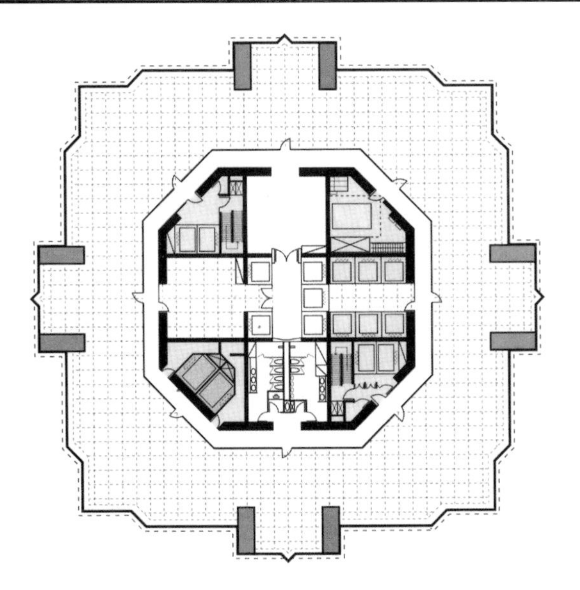

The fourth tallest skyscraper in the world is designed with an architectural style that conjures up the style of Chinese pagodas through the use of overlapping roofs. The reference is stylized. At every recurrence, upside down in relation to pagoda roofs and jutting out much less, there is a slight tapering of the body of the building. As the building rises, the recurrences move closer together, and the top is pyramid-like. On the top 35 stories, there is an internal open space going through all the floors like a huge well. The Jinmao Building is one of the most significant buildings of mixed architecture between the West and China both in old and modern Shanghai.

GOLDEN FINANCE TOWER

高登金融大厦

Yan'an Dong Lu (between Bund/ Waitan and Sichuan Zhong Lu)
Huangpu District
黄浦区延安东路(外滩和四川中路之间)
Date: Completed 1999
Function: Office

8

Parallelepiped tower, the facades take up the facades of the nearby Shanghai Sports Club built in the 1930s. (see Itinerary 1-1)

SHANGHAI CENTRAL PLAZA

上海中环广场

381, Huaihai Zhong Lu
Luwan District
卢湾区淮海中路 381 号
Date: 1999
Function: Office and Shopping Mall

9

The second example (after the Garden Hotel) where the existing building is restored — even if completely transformed — and becomes the base for the new high-rise bldg. built above it.

SHANGHAI PUDONG INTERNATIONAL AIRPORT (SPIA)

上海浦东国际机场

Date: Completed 1999 (First Phase)

Design: ADP(France)+ECADI(Shanghai)

Function: International Airport

10

The completed part is one fourth of the whole airport project. The master plan, in symmetrical and geometric layout, consists in four identical airport quays; in the centre an artificial rectangular shape lake and the highway and railway leading to the city centre. The architecture is like the world wide "engineering esthetic".

CIRCUS WORLD
上海马戏世界

2266, Gonghe Xin Lu
(between Daning Lu and Guangzhong Lu)
Zhabei District
闸北区共和新路 2266 号
(大宁路和广中路之间)
Date: Completed 1999
Design:ECADI(Shanghai)
Function:entertainment

11

Three buildings joined together by a central podium square. The whole complex recalls Le Courbusier's architectures.

PLAZA 66
恒隆广场

1266, Nanjing Xi Lu
Jing'an District
静安区南京西路 1266 号
Date: Completed 2001
Design: KPF (USA)+ECADI (Shanghai)
Function: Office and Shopping Mall

12

Two skyscrapers (at the moment only one built), one taller with 66 stories and base. Simple design.

JIUSHI TOWER
久事大厦

Zhongshan Dong Er Lu (corner Dongmen Lu)
Huangpu District (formerly Nanshi District)
南市区中山东二路(东门路路口)
Date: Completed 2001
Design: Norman Foster Ass.
(England)+ECADI (Shanghai)
Function: Office

13

Tower on corner, curved facade facing north; double glass skin, three loggias with internal gardens for a more natural (not just mechanical) air-conditioning system according to the new architectural theories from UK.

TOMORROW SQUARE
明天广场

399, Nanjing Xi Lu (corner Huangpi Bei Lu)
Huangpu District
黄浦区南京西路 399 号（黄陂北路路口）
Date: Completed 2002
Design: J. PORTMAN ASS. (USA)
Function: Office, Hotel

14

Skyscraper as landmark beside the People's Square in Huangpu District. Impressive architecture: volume's shape and top like a missile, a sphere into the open air top.

15

◀ **BUND FINANCE CENTRE**

外滩中心

Henan Zhong Lu
(corner Yan'an Dong Lu)
Huangpu District
黄浦区河南中路(延安东路路口)
Date: 2002
Design: J. PORTMAN ASS.(USA)
Function: Office, Residential

The third high-rise in the city designed by the American architect J. Portman. Layout resembles the Shanghai Centre but facing west. The top — in the second and final project — is an impressive and playful hat.

16

▼ **16. CIRO'S PLAZA**

仙乐斯广场

388, Nanjing Xi Lu (corner Huangpi Bei Lu)
Huangpu District
黄浦区南京西路388号(黄陂北路路口)
Date: 2002
Design: HLW Architects (USA)
Function: Office, Commercial

Tower building situated along the circular perimeter of People's Square, Geometric volumes tilted and rotated. Interesting modern architecture, no impressive and no monumental.

17

WORLD FINANCE CENTRE

上海国际环球金融中心

(Under Construction)
Pudong Lujiazui, Pudong New Area
浦东陆家嘴浦东新区
Design: KPF(USA)+MORI BIRU (Japan)+SHIMIEU+SHMIZU (Japan)+ECADI(Shanghai)
Function: Office, Hotel

It will be the tallest bldg. in the world; monholitic volume changing shape from the bottom to the top: from a square plan to a rectangular plan on the diagonal; huge hole on the top; simple design.

The complex consists of a square in the middle and two buildings in a geometric lay-out determined by two axes. The east/west axis runs from Pudong Lujiazui Area to the new Century Central Park. The north/south axis goes from the Pudong Government Building on the north side of the square to the Museum/Congress Building on the south side of the square. The second one will be the Science Museum consisting of six sections (astronomic, biological, prehistoric, etc.) and a congress hall. The whole complex recalls the esplanades in modern Paris like the Defense District and the Tres Grand Bibliotheque.

SCIENCE CITY

18

上海科技馆

Yang Gao Nan Lu, Pu Dong
浦东杨高南路
Date: Completed 2001
Design: RTKL(USA)
+ECADI(Shanghai)
Function: Museum, Congress

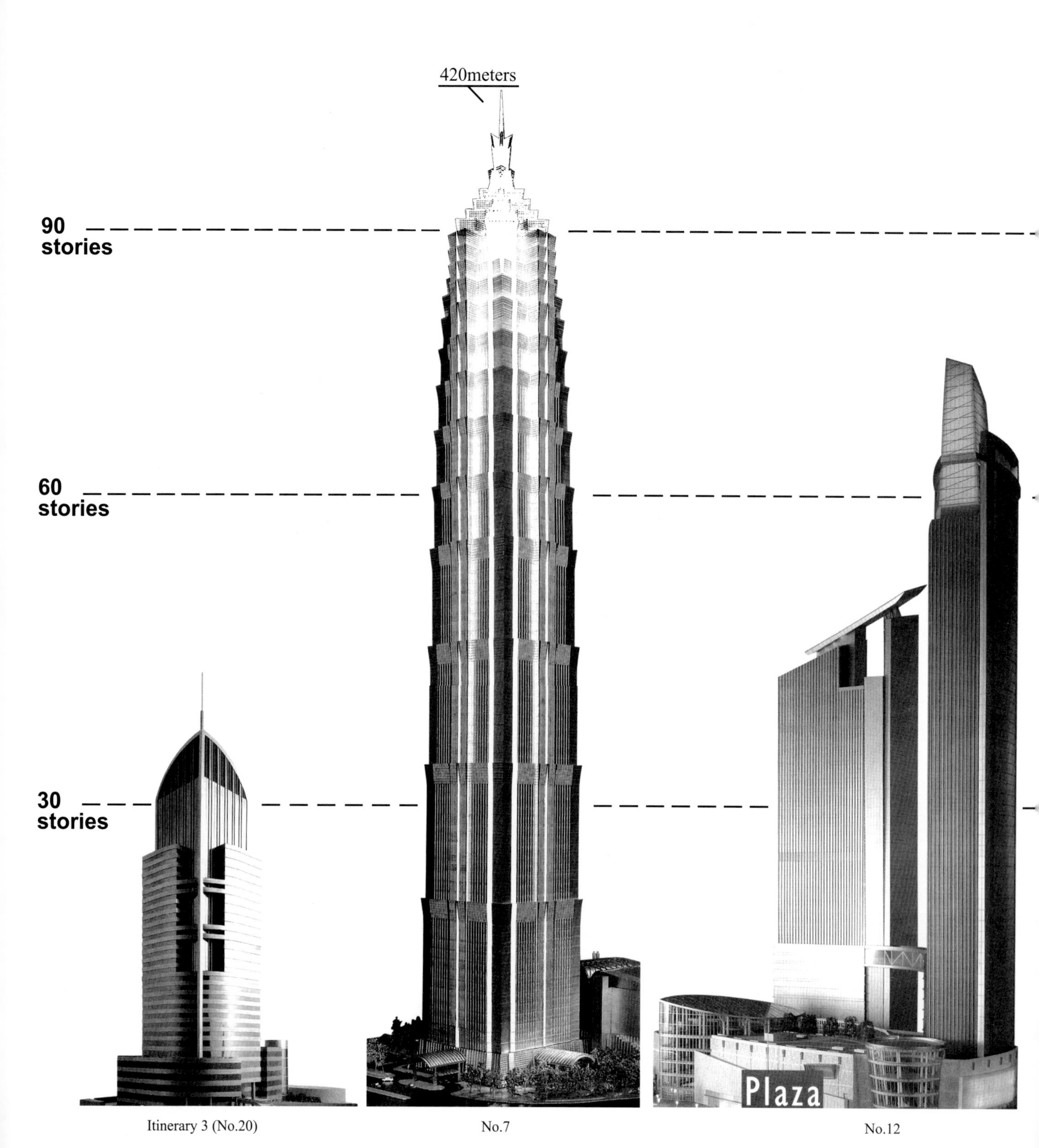

Itinerary 3 (No.20)

No.7

No.12

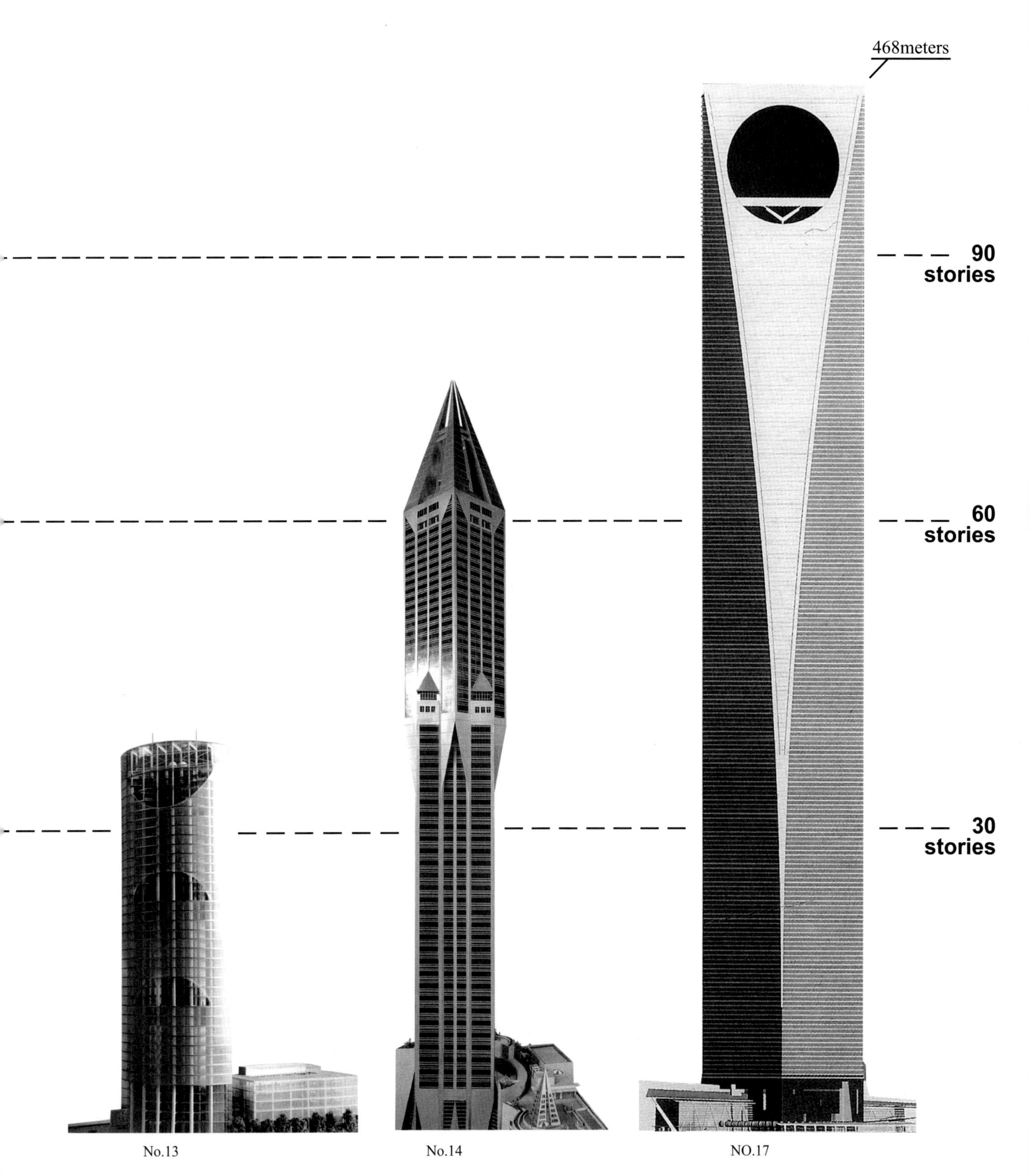
468meters
90
stories
60
stories
30
stories
No.13
No.14
NO.17

New Areas

PUDONG NEW AREA

浦东新区

New Area for Financial Activities

Construction Date: **FROM 1992**

Function: **IN THE AREA THERE ARE SHANGHAI STOCK EXCHANGE, OFFICE BUILDINGS, HOTELS, RESIDENTIAL BUILDINGS, SHOPPING CENTRES, ETC.**

▲ China Insurance Building ▲ Shanghai Information Tower ▲ Shanghai Pudong Development Bank Building ▲ Bank of China Tower ▲ Bocom Financial Tower

▲ Huaneng Union Building ▲ World Financial Building

▲ China Merchants Tower ▲ China Insurance Building

Shanghai Stock Exchange Building

▲ Chia Tai Commercial Center ▲ Pudong Custom House

Hongqiao Development Zone

HONGQIAO DEVELOPMENT ZONE

虹桥开发区

New Area for International Activities

Construction Date: **FROM 1980S**

Function: **IN THE AREA THERE ARE OFFICE BUILDINGS, HOTELS, RESIDENTIAL BUILDINGS, FOREIGN COMSULATES, SHOPPING CENTRES, EXHIBITION CENTRES, ETC.**

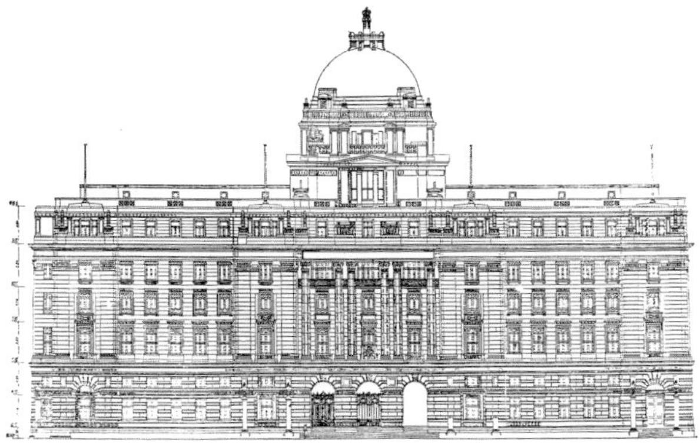

B) Renovation and Reconstruction

1

Renovation and restoration of one of the most important building in 1920s and 1930s. Western Neo-classic style. Interior is in Roman typology and style. Mosaics probably by Italians.

SHANGHAI PUDONG DEVELOPMENT BANK

上海浦东发展银行

formerly Municipal Government Building
formerly Hongkong and Shanghai Banking Corporation
10-12, Zhongshan Dong Yi Lu
Huangpu District (Bund/Waitan)
黄浦区外滩中山东一路 10-12 号
Date: Original construction 1923 (Itinerary 3-6)
Renovation 1999
Function: Office

SHANGHAI ART MUSEUM

上海美术馆

formerly Shanghai Library
formerly Jockey Club Building
325, Nanjing Xi Lu (corner Huangpi Bei Lu)
Huangpu District
黄浦区南京西路 325 号(黄陂北路路口)
Date: Original construction 1928 by MOORHEAD and HALSE
Renovation: 1999
Function: Art exposition space

2

Renovation and restoration of one of the most significant buildings in 1920s and 1930s: the former Jockey Club Building inside the Hippodrome. Eclectic architecture: bell tower, Tuscany columns, wooden boiserie in the interiors.

SITE OF THE FIRST NATIONAL CONGRESS OF THE COMMUNIST PARTY OF CHINA

中国共产党一大会址

76, Xingye Lu
Luwan District (corner Huangpi Nan Lu)
卢湾区兴业路 76 号(黄陂南路路口)
Date: Original construction 1910s (Longtang House)
First renovation 1951
Renovation+Addition 1999
Function: Museum

3

Renovation and new addition building for the traditional Shikumen house where the First Congress of the Chinese Communist Party took place: it was the home of one of the founder members of the Chinese Communist Party.

Longhua New Town is a complex of new buildings in Chinese traditional style surrounding the existing Pagoda, in front of the south entrance of the Temple.

4

LONGHUA NEW TOWN

龙华镇

(Longhua Temple and Longhua Pagoda)
(龙华寺 龙华塔)
2853, Longhua Lu
Xuhui District
徐汇区龙华路 2853 号
Date: Longhua Temple
First construction: 242.A.D Rebuilt: 1403-1420
Existing structures: 1875-1899
Longhua Pagoda
First construction: 247 A.D Existing structure: 977 A.D
Longhua New Town: completed 1999
Function: In the area there are a Buddhist temple, shopping malls, places of entertainment, and a museum. etc.

5

Reconstruction of traditional buildings and streets in the area of the Old Chinese City.

CHINESE OLD CITY

老城隍庙

Fang Bang Lu
Nanshi District
南市区方浜路
Date: Renovation and reconstruction from 1950s (the Tea House) to 1999
Function: Commercial Centre

Renovation and a new addition of two blocks of traditional Shikumen houses. Due to the complete function transformation, the traditional structures and layout had been heavily transformed. Pedestrian streets resemble those in the historical European cities.

6 XINTIANDI AREA

新天地

Huangpi Nan Lu / Madang Lu between Taicang Lu / Zizhong Lu

Luwan District

卢湾区黄陂南路 / 马当路 太仓路 / 自忠路

Construction Date: Existing Houses 1910s/1920s

Renovation and new buildings 1999/2001

Function: Commercial, Retail, Exhibition, Entertainment, Apartment

SHANGHAI RAILWAY STATION

铁路上海站

Tianmu Xi Lu (corner Hengfeng Bei Lu)
Zhabei District
闸北区天目西路(恒丰北路路口)
Date: Original construction 1987 by ECADI, Shanghai
Renovation 2000

Renovation and restyling of the main facade (south) ,main entrance and the passenger atrium, from a socialistic architecture to an international high-tech one. Enlargement of main entrance and the passenger atrium.

Itinerary 5

Shanghai People's Square

People's Square is the symbol of modern Shanghai in terms of its location and history. In recent years, it has undergone a drastic renovation and many landmark buildings were added around it.

This vast open space used to house the Hippodrome during the foreign concession period in the International Settlement. After the Revolution in 1949 citizens used to assemble in this vast and entirely building-free area.

Now the centre of this area contains the most important public buildings of the city: the City Hall, completed in 1994; the Shanghai Museum, completed in 1995; the New Shanghai Grand Theatre, completed in 1998; the Urban Planning Exhibition Centre completed in 1999.

Three Generations of Public Buildings in Shanghai

The new square in the centre of the city is symbolic of the changes occurring in Shanghai.

During the foreign concession period, Shanghai municipal administrative offices were located outside the city centre — in the Yangpu District on the north of Foreign Settlements — and modern constructions were built in traditional Chinese style (Neo-classic Chinese): the Government Bldg., the Museum, the Stadium and the Library (see Itinerary 1-18).

After 1949, the city regained its Chinese connotations, and public offices were moved to foreign constructed buildings (French or English) in more central areas.

The Municipal Government offices were first in the former Shanghai Municipal Council Building at Hankou Lu, later moved to the former HongKong & Shanghai Banking Corporation Bldg. on the Bund/Waitan till 1994 (see Itinerary 3-6; Itinerary 4-1B).

The museum was in a French style building in Yan'an Lu — Zhong Hui Building. (see Itinerary 1-13) — from 1959 to 1995.

For the theatre, the first generation consists of traditional Chinese theatres, an important example of which is situated in the residence of a mandarin —Yu Yuan Garden in the old city, going back to the Ming and Qing dynasties (from 15th century to the beginning of the last century). The second generation coincides with the foreign concession period in Shanghai, during which many theatres and cinemas were built, run by major international film companies. The third generation is represented by the present-day Shanghai Grand Theatre in the People's Square.

Also the Municipal Library — now in Huaihai Zhong Lu (see Itinerary 4-5) — moved from the north to the former Jockey Club Building (see Itinerary 4-2B) in the centre of the city, till 1996.

Among them the Theatre is the most representative and symbolic. The first generation follows the Chinese tradition. The second generation is only in Western tradition. The third generation is a mixture of Chinese and Western traditions.

The traditional Chinese theatres were mostly built in the houses and gardens of the rich and the powerful.They consisted of a square or rectangular courtyard, with a two-storied colonnade running along one side for the small audience. The stage was on one side of the courtyard, in a very forward position, raised on a platform and with a cover unrelated to the colonnade.

The theatres and cinemas in the foreign concession period were of Western type, of Greek and Roman inspiration, and quite unlike traditional Chinese theatres, they had a slightly sloping large auditorium rectangular or trapezoidal in shape, an upper balcony, a raised stage and a single covering, with a large foyer/entrance. The architecture was also Western in style, although designed by Chinese designers, with the adoption of neo-classical ideas (the Nanjing Theatre, now the Shanghai Music Hall), a sense of Italian Renaissance (the Lyceum Theatre), modernist style (Grand Theatre, see Itinerary 1-22) or art-Deco (Paramount Theatre and Majestic Theatre).

The present Shanghai Grand Theatre was designed by a French architect with the collaboration of the Architectural Insitute of Shanghai. The architecture is mixed. The tipology is from the Western tradition. The location follows the Western tradition — in the main square — but in a Chinese planning — facing south.

People's Square: A Chinese Urban Space

With the combination of different functions and styles the square would be typical of the Western tradition were it not for a significant difference: the buildings around it all face south, in accordance with Chinese tradition. So it lacks the quality of a spatial hollow created by the relationship between the buildings and the open square itself. The buildings do not face each others across the square, they do not look all onto the central space, but all face one way: south.

The buildings are oriented with the facade and entrance pointing southwards. They are based on a rigid symmetry. This means that the four constructions are perfectly in line and parallel. And this is the fact, in terms of layout and city planning, that does not give this setting the sense of a spatial basin defined by the relationship between constructions and the emptiness around them as the Western square tradition is (from the Italian *piazza* and the ancient Roman *forum* and ancient Greece *agora'*).

The Shanghai Grand Theatre , the City Hall, the Urban Planning Exhibition Centre are in a row behind the Shanghai Museum: the whole takes on the form of an open T pointing southwards (or it probably resembles the Chinese character "zhong", meaning centre). The Museum's main entrance (with sculptures of guard animals) is on the south side, meaning that it does not face the central area, though there is a fountain between the City Hall and the Museum itself.

Also other main buildings — as important landmark around the square — are facing south and not towards the open space: the Telecomminication Bldg. and the Harbour Ring Plaza skyscraper (see Itinerary 3-20) follow the Chinese traditional lay-out.

All buildings look southwards, their facades and their entrances turned towards the south. Therefore, they have no relations with the square, nor with the past. Nothing reminds of what the place was like before the latest renovation. The old buildings along Nanjing Xi Lu, the Jockey Club Building and the Moore Memorial Church are not connected anymore with the main urban space between the new public buildings. The four public buildings have relation only with the south.

This kind of lay-out is similar to the Longtang house, to that of the modern residential blocks and also to the model for all of these constructions: the Forbidden City in Beijing. "Terraced" and "aligned" constructions that have their facade and entrance pointing to the same direction. In these construction blocks the most important element is the very orientation of the buildings. This means that they "must" be aligned and parallel. There isn't any urban relation.

So that the main square of Shanghai is thus symbolic of the ongoing architectural and city-planning trends in China, reflecting the past and recent times. Whatever the style and function of a building, its orientation and alignment have already been decided. This construction method has become a very rigid rule that has proved stronger than any demand from the historical period or building locality. It is such a strong rule that it can accommodate any architectural style or construction technique, which usually become simple external coverings.

▲ **People's Square in 1920s/1930s was the Hippodrome**

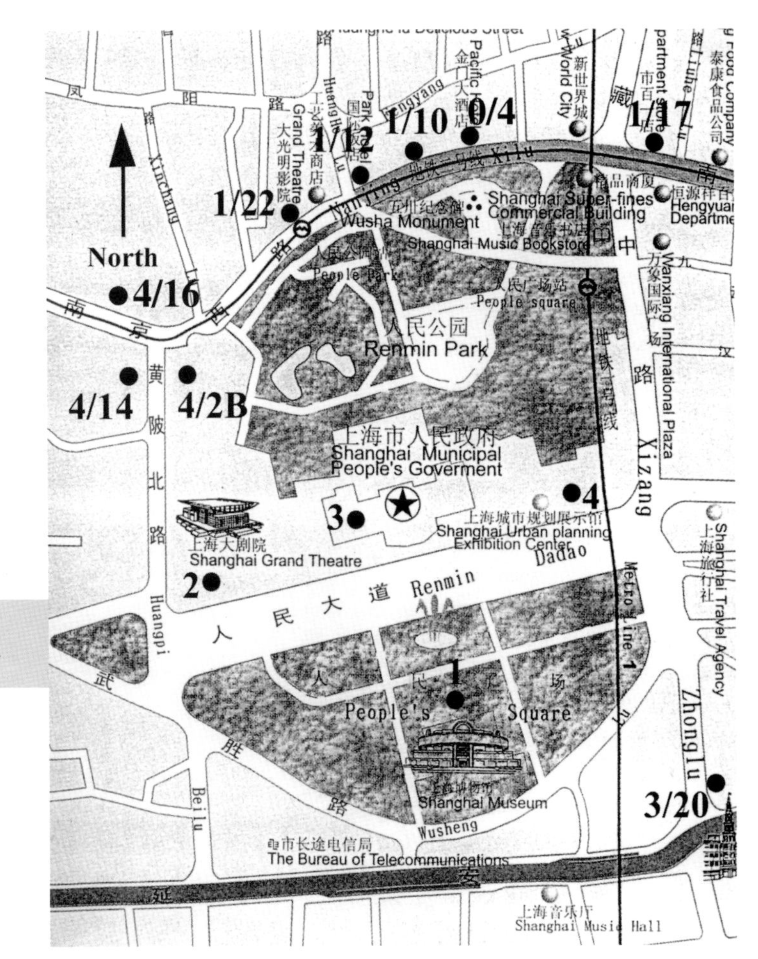

▼ People's Square today from Harbour Ring Plaza

SHANGHAI MUSEUM

上海博物馆

Design: Shanghai Architectural Institute directed by Mr Xing Tonghe

Date: 1995

1

The Museum is located opposite the City Hall. It deliberately and expressly takes up the shape of ancient bronze tripods with handles, while the top part of the building, circular with a skylight at the center, takes the shape of an ancient bronze mirror of the Han dynasty.

SHANGHAI GRAND THEATRE

上海大剧院

Design: J. Charpentier/Arte, France + ECADI, Shanghai
Date: 1998

The volume of the Grand Theatre mirrors the sweep of the roofs and division into three sections — tripartition — typical of classic Chinese buildings. The horizontal axis are predominant. Its key feature is the large curved roof, concave skywards, suspended and detached from the body below. The three sections are the base, central block and a large roof borne up on pillars, between which the walls are simple panels. The typology is from the Western tradition. The main auditorium has extensive stalls, two stories of galleries and three stories of balconies. The effect is very stylish and offers a very different image from that offered by Shanghai Museum's references to the past. The Theatre is one of the most significant buildings of mixed architecture between the West and China both in the old and modern Shanghai.

2

THE CITY HALL

上海市人大常委会、上海市政府

Design: Shanghai Architectural Design Institute

Date: 1996

3

The City Hall building is a 15-story parallelepiped building having a large avant-corps entrance and symmetrical portico and facade. The outside appearance is regular, with small square windows.

The Urban Planning Exhibition Centre is a compact and double symmetrical volume covered by four open, upside-down pyramid sections in white aluminum panels. Under the roof there is an amphitheatric-shape open-air terrace.

THE URBAN PLANNING EXHIBITION CENTRE

城市规划展示馆

Design: ECADI, Shanghai

Date: 1999

Three Generations of Theatre Buildings

1ST GENERATION

Traditional Chinese Theatre

▲ Yu Yuan Garden Theatre

Shanghai Grand Theatre in 1990s ▼

3RD GENERATION

Mixed Architecture between the West and China

Shanghai Music Hall in 1930s(Nanking Theatre) ▶

Lyceum Theatre in 1930s ▼

2ND GENERATION

Western Style Cinemas and Theatres

Three Generations of Museums

FIRST GENERATION

Shanghai Museum in 1930s In Yangpu District by Dong Dayou

THIRD GENERATION

Shanghai Museum in 1990s

SECOND GENERATION

Shanghai Museum since 1950s to the beginning of 1990s

Four Generations of Public Administration Buildings

FIRST GENERATION

Public Administration Building at Hankou Road Designed by R.C. Turner

SECOND GENERATION

Public Administration Building at Jiangwan in 1930s

THIRD GENERATION

Public Administration Building since 1950s to the beginning of 1990s

FOURTH GENERATION

Public Administration Building in 1990s

Appendix 1

Landscaped Level, Landscaped Ground and Landscaped Sky in Shanghai

Appendix 2

Wandering and Wondering about both Bund\Waitan and People's Square

Appendix 1

Landscaped Level, Landscaped Ground And Landscaped Sky In Shanghai

Shanghai is the world's newest and most radical metropolis. It possesses the impetuous charm of dizzy and unstoppable growth combined with the unhidden and deep charm of size. Its appeal is explicit, visible, recognizable in its outward appearance; the out-of-scale size of its architecture, the verticality of residential buildings, the elevated highway, the pastel colours of the skyscrapers and malls — towering above the small "islands" of the former concessions and the other dark and silent areas. The signs of the very recent metamorphosis can be seen in the city's fascinating landscape; more than 3,000 skyscrapers, built in only 8 years and all over 100 metres in height, outline the skyline of this metropolis, stretching as far as the horizon.

Unlike Los Angeles, where millions of light unceasingly cover the boundless urban territory, Shanghai night lighting forms a wing which rises towards the sky and makes it lighter.

The reformation process — started in 1978 by Deng Xiaoping — revolutionised the city's stagnant economy. It was Deng who reinvigorated the economies of the coastal provinces by starting the Special Economic Zones (SEZ) in order to integrate the Chinese market with the international market; these were aimed at creating a fertile ground for Shanghai's entrance into the world. In 1984, the idea of developing the Pudong area took shape. In 1990, the government decided to start building, through a new SEZ on the east bank of the Huangpu River. In 1992, Pudong was chosen to become the business and financial centre of East Asia, the dragon's head of the Chinese economy.

Shanghai as a contemporary city is built on these foundations. Its charming landscape has a liquid beauty because, despite the verticality of its architecture, it doesn't resemble New York, which is compressed into a rigid and systematic grid. Shanghai has the sinuosity of the snake-like big river, the Huangpu. It has skyscrapers and towers which are arranged on non-rectangular sites, along streets built on complex lines, also including known urban structures, but always restyled into more linguistic forms, not repeating the same models, and incorporating exotic designs. Shanghai doesn't have architecture with dominating facades, architecture that is monumental or symbolic; it has very few buildings of power, its architectural elements don't emphasize its history. Since 1990, theatres, auditoriums, shopping malls, conference centres, cinemas, video game arcades, restaurants, art galleries, have been accommodated within the new architecture, in new cultural and sports structures which always offer a variety of functions and activities. Homes are a part of the towers. Underground stations can become part of the new plazas and pedestrian streets have room for open-air amphitheatres. A thriving urban quality emerges, challenging the superiority of modernism held until a short time ago by western metropolises.

The image for the new Millennium has been entrusted to a big project that covers the entire Lujiazui District in the Pudong area. According to plan, the projects should look like a modified version of New York, Hong Kong and Tokyo put together. Opposite the Bund/Waitan, where the first riverwalk runs by the oldest skyscrapers, bank headquarters and hotels, a new splendid promenade lines the area. The remarkable architecture of Pudong is the new image created by economic liberalisation. Before 1990, the area was scattered with warehouses and industrial sheds. Today, the highest skyscrapers are being built. These very sophisticated architectures are the result of state commissions, entrusting the most prestigious works (urban plans, cultural institutions, sports facilities) to architects of international fame — whereas private operators deal much less with the appearance of their buildings.

In Pudong there are expected to be three main skyscrapers, surrounded by a further 50 towers (150-250m). The deck of the Jin Mao Tower (421m) — a magnificent skyscraper — and the Oriental Pearl TV Tower (468m) are key domestic tourist destinations. They look out over big shopping centres, the most sophisticated restaurants and new theatres. The new projects are suitable for numerous activities and urban entertainments. One of the most elaborate is that created by Norman Foster, the Jiushi Tower (168m). The Shanghai Information Center by Nikken Sekkei (202m) will become a telecommunications office. Under construction is the World Financial Center (460m) by Kohn/Pedersen/Fox (KPF), which is also a multipurpose building. But Pudong is also a residential area, with elegant complexes made up of apartment buildings and villas, which surround the golf driving range and overlook the river. These complexes are composed of towers, semicircular buildings that bound the internal courtyards, by terraced houses and small villas. The styles imitate English cottages, French maisons and a few Italian banisters. They play with imitations also from the old Lilong, Longtang or Siheyuan houses. The contamination of styles in Shanghai reflects the international dimension of this free port dating back to 1840 and to the 11 historic areas designated as landmarks.

The new Shanghai is colourful, bright, full of electronic elements, decorated pavements and huge screens. The new Shanghai has reduced its overcrowding, and is wiping out urban poverty, bringing down ultra-conservatism and destroying identities built over the centuries. The western media describe this very rapid construction as a catastrophic and bizarre scenario, where the fast pace of creations threatens to destroy social and productive organisation or worse still the historic testimonials of violence and the Western powers. In short, criticism moves beneath the ghostly image of Eastern creations as second-rate realisations.

To all-out critics of the Chinese scene (but especially of the many new urban projects) fetishes continue to be manifested and meaningless structures continue to be built. Criticism concerns the lack of authenticity of many of the new accomplishments (skyscrapers, plazas, tunnels, bridges, residential structures, garden cities, etc.). Finally "the inventors of the enemy" demonise the money which destroys the romantic urban worlds of the past. Different is the view of the Dutch architect Rem Koolhaas who compares western observers to relatives of the dead who continue to complain about a wasted heritage. But where is the romanticism of misery and overcrowding, of the lack of drains, lack of sanitation in the terrace houses of the former concession areas and in the Old City, of urban zones that are thoroughly unhealthy, unliveable and lacking in air (as the East End in London in 1887 examined by Charles Booth)? And considering the matter in the opposite way, but completely symmetrically, why should urban renewal, pedestrian streets, stations and brand constructions be interpreted as a false front, as superficial embellishments, as inhuman spaces or imitations of unreal worlds? The huge Renmin or People's Square after sunset is filled with people. In front of the Shanghai Museum, hundreds of couples dance to the rhythm of their portable radios as a new urban custom, a completely spontaneous and informal custom that is combined with the *taiji* gymnastics in the morning. The out-of-scale size of the square — set on different levels, covered with flowerbeds and fountains crossed by children — does not arouse sensations associated with being amazed at the sublime. It gives a merry image of urban life, less authoritative than that of Tian'anmen Square, and carries out its function as the central place of the city. Under it is a shopping centre and an underground station. All of this is dominated by important administrative institutions such as the offices of the Municipality and the cultural departments — the Shanghai Grand Theatre, the Shanghai Art Museum and Shanghai Museum.

Shanghai is not an empty picture. It has more than 15,000 foreign companies compared with 6,000 in Hong Kong. In recent years, the banks and management of multinationals have moved here from the major financial centre of Hong Kong, and at the same time the government is encouraging companies with a national focus to be localised in the area of Pudong. The most elegant homes are marked out for the executives of foreign businesses, who have much higher salaries than the national average. For ten years, the housing market has been open for sales and for rent, and companies, both international and domestic, have been building residential complexes everywhere. The new sector policies have a particular Asian style similar to the urban policies of Singapore and a few Japanese organisational systems. The growing tolerance of the Chinese government for individual freedom and free expression can also be noted. The Internet is a factor; cybercafés, galleries and exhibition halls, cultural events such as the Art Biennial, discos, cinemas and shopping centres are the places most visited by young people who look for sharply defined experiences. Shanghai people are now experiencing a freedom they never had before, and the expression of joy can be seen in faces full of wonder when they visit the new architectures, enter malls, walk and play in the open spaces of the brand new Shanghai. The drive along overpasses — bordered with green areas — to the Pudong new airport provides a wonderful bird's eye tour over the city, dizzily passing by playgrounds and low houses, running at a height of 35m, landing in a blue airport and taking off above a mirror of clear water.

by Ms Mara Memo

Professor of Urban Sociology at "La Sapienza" University No.1, Rome

Appendix 2

Wandering and Wondering about both Bund\Waitan and People's Square

As written in this book, in Shanghai there are both Western and Chinese architecture elements. In some situations they integrate each other, in other situations they are one beside the other. In a short distance of one mile, the Bund/Waitan waterfront and People's Square represent two different urban concepts: West the Bund and China the People's Square.

I explained in this guide that it is not the style of the buildings that makes the difference between the two areas. The style of the buildings on the Bund/Waitan is from Western historical heritage. The style of the four public buildings in the People's Square is a Chinese interpretation of international and modern theories.

Even the two historical periods are not enough to explain those differences: buildings along the Bund were built during Foreign Settlement in the 1930s and the People's Square was constructed after Liberation and reconstructed in late 1990s.

What is or what are the urban concepts and elements that determine the differences? Since my first visit to Shanghai in April 1992, I wondered a lot about this question. In that period People's Square did not exist as it is nowadays. On the other hand the Bund/Waitan was already a historical heritage. In preparing this guide I visited, I wandered and I came back many times in both places in different periods of the year, in different moments of the day and night, under different weather situations. I noticed and watched each element that could enlighten me. I went in both places also for personal reasons: alone, with my daughter or with friends.

The second question is: Why I feel well in the Bund/Waitan and why I feel unwell in the People's Square? Why I like to have a walk along the waterfront of the Bund and I don't like that much to stroll in the People's Square?

Walking on the bank of the Bund/Waitan — on one side the bustling Huangpu River, on the other side the 1930s monumental buildings — and enjoying the big view eastward to Pudong — both as a farmland in 1992 and as a modern metropolis filled with new towers and skyscrapers since 1995 — I always enjoy this urban area. Why?

The Western style of the buildings could be one reason. Those styles are familiar to me. These buildings are "copies" of the original and older ones in Europe. As an Italian I know the original examples spreading in the whole Europe. It's said that the Shanghai waterfront recalls the Liverpool waterfront. Another reason could be the bustling traffic along the Huangpu River. But this is not an architectural reason, even if it could enrich the urban space. One more reason could be the view towards the modern skyscrapers in Pudong. But they didn't exist at all in 1992. The reason is the urban concept that founded the waterfront's lay-out.

The urban concept comes from the Western tradition. It is the same of waterfronts, squares and streets backdrops in the European cities. Due to the relation between the edifices and the void, the array of buildings creates an urban space (a spatial basin). The array follows the natural loop of the river so that there is a deep relation between the manmade elements and the natural site. The urban space is indelibly tied up with that site. This is what made this area familiar to me regardless of the styles of the edifices.

On the other hand, walking and wandering in People's Square, I asked myself why I didn't feel well in that urban space. Why? Maybe because it is not familiar to me? This is not the reason: many non-familiar places could make strangers feel comfortable, too. Maybe because the square is new and it has not yet acquired the "dust" of the history. Of course not, I'm not nostalgic at all. And then, again why? There are public buildings like many European squares: the Theatre, the Museum, the City Hall, the Urban Planning Building and a fountain in the centre. I watched and watched again. Then I noticed the perfect alignment of these buildings, their same orientation to south, their layout regardless of the site and its history, the big avenue crossing the area without connection to other city roads, the main entrance of the Museum not facing the other buildings and neither the void between them. What does it mean? Which kind of lay-out is this? I don't know anything like this.

Even the buildings built in different times around the square are not facing the square itself. Why the Harbour Ring Plaza, built in the turn of the century, doesn't "face" the square but the corner between Xizang Road and Yan'an Road in a southward direction? And why the Post and Telecomunication Building, built in the 1970s, faces the south and not the former People's Park? Finally I got the answer: the answer is, it follows the concept of the Forbidden City in Beijing. The whole complex of the Imperial Palace has a relation only with the south: the main axis, the main facades, the entrance gates, the numerous courtyards. The Forbidden City is an "enclave" in the centre of the city. Also the traditional houses in whole China face south. The Buddha's images face south too. The temple's lay out have relation with the south too. The modern public buildings face south too. This makes those sites not familiar to me: both the urban spaces and architectural complexes.

At this moment I got the answer to my second questions (or first ones, it depends): Why I feel well in the Bund/Waitan and why I feel unwell in the People's Square? Why I like to have a walk along the waterfront of the Bund and I don't like to enjoy strolling in the People's Square? Because the first one is familiar to me and the latter is not familiar: this is not the answer. There is something deeper and stronger that found those urban spaces and architecture complexes. I go on in my speculation!

Due to the relation between the array of the

buildings and the river's loop, the Bund/Waitan waterfront is an urban space in a "human scale". The European (and Italian) Humanism ideas founded this space. Man is the centre of this space and the point of reference in dimensional, proportional and composition of the whole area. The manmade edifices follow the natural site: joined together they create an urban spatial basin. The centrality of man means that there may arise spatial, linguistic and temporal differences. This is what makes me feel well walking, wandering and enjoying the Huangpu waterfront.

And on the contrary, why do I feel unwell in the People's Square? The buildings' alignment and their southward direction have no relation with the site. The lay-out is unrelated with the area. It has relation with the sun. You can "move" the four buildings, the fountain and the avenue anywhere else: everything remains the same. The area is "open" to the sky. The composition seems dictated by laws that trascend a given historical period, everlasting laws beyond the human sphere of action: laws of nature and of sun.

These are the differences between the two main important urban spaces in Shanghai. Or at least they are my impressions. This is what makes modern Shanghai so great and fascinating: the coexistence of different urban spaces.

Luigi Novelli

Bibliography for Itineraries 1-2-3

- Wu Jiang, *The History of Shanghai Architecture, 1840-1949*
  Tongji University Press, 1997 (Chinese)
- Luo Xiaowei, Wu Jiang, *Shanghai Longtang*
  Shanghai People's Fine Arts Publishing House, 1997 (Chinese and English)
- Luo Xiaowei, Tongji University, *A Guide to Shanghai Architecture*
  Shanghai People's Fine Arts Publishing House, 1996 (Chinese and English)
- Guobo, photographer, *The Fast Vanishing Shanghai Lanes*
  Shanghai Pictorial Publishing House, 1996 (Chinese, English and Japanese)
- *Tour of Shanghai Historical Architecture*
  Henan Fine Arts Publishing House, 1994 (Chinese, English and Japanese)
- *Controspazio n.3,* May/June 1992 monograph on Shanghai
  By Arch. Corrado Minervini, Turin and Prof. Zheng Shiling, Shanghai
  Gangemi Editore, Reggio Calabria1992 (Italian)
- Chen Congzhou, Tongji University,
  The History of Modern Architecture in Shanghai
  Shanghai Sanlian Press, 1988 (Chinese)

Language Translation Notes

In this book, Pinyin is used for special names; Pinyin is the transliteration of Chinese characters into Roman letters. The following are some examples of the translation from Pinyin to English:

Lu = Road
Bei = North　　Nan = South
Zhong= Central　　Dong = East
Xi = West

Longtang =a lane lined and terraced with residential houses
Shikumen = a style of houses having a wooden door with stone frames

Yi = One　　Er = Two　　Xizang = Tibet

Names Note:

- Names of some buildings could be different now due to the change of owners, management and function

Publisher: Zhang Ruizhi
Author: Luigi Novelli
Edition Editor: Lily Lijuan Zhou
Finalization: Eric Lock
Cover Design & Layout: Sinomedia

Shanghai Architecture Guide

Published by Haiwen Audio — Video Publishers
Printed by Yanzhong Printing House
Distributed by Shanghai Book Traders
390 Fuzhou Road, Shanghai 200001, China
First Edition: February, 2003
First Printing: February, 2003

Author's Notes:

Text and photos by the author. Totally 199 photos, 23 drawings for 130 buildings / complexes and 5 maps.

Except photos:
page 6 — page 10 — page 11 — page 14 (No. 2-No.4 -No.5) — page 16 (No. 2) — page 17 (No. 7) — page 18 — page 66 — page 74 — page 76 — page 77 — page 84 (No. 1 right-No.2 left) — page 87 — page 96 — page 99 — page 102 (top right)— page 108 (left) — page 110 — page 111 — page 113 — page 114 — page 115— page 116 — page 118 (top) — page 119 (top)